WHAT'S
a good tree
WRONG
cannot bring forth
WITH
evil fruit
MORMONS?

B. JAY GLADWELL

Cold Tree Press
Nashville, Tennessee

This work is not an official publication of The Church of Jesus Christ of Latter-day Saints. The views expressed herein are the responsibility of the author and do not necessarily represent the position of the Church.

Published by Cold Tree Press, Nashville, Tennessee

For information regarding permission, write to:
Cold Tree Press, 214 Overlook Court, Suite 253, Brentwood, Tennessee 37027.

Library of Congress Number: 2008930257
Cover Photos:
©iStockphoto.com/ Christine Balderas

ISBN-13: 978-1-58385-279-8
ISBN-10: 1-58385-279-4

Come now, and let us reason together, saith the Lord.

—Isaiah 1:18

Produce your cause, saith the LORD;
bring forth your strong reasons.

—Isaiah 41:21

Contents

Preface

We've all been taught from practically day one not to discuss politics or religion. In this book, we will not be discussing politics.

Since you're reading this book, it's presumed that you (1) have a belief in a Supreme Being, God; and (2) you believe that Jesus is the Christ—the Savior and Redeemer of mankind. So, with that in mind, let me ask you: if you wanted to know more about someone's religious beliefs, who would you ask?

Imagine yourself living in Jerusalem at the time of Christ. You hear about this man—this prophet—named Jesus, who teaches "as one having authority, and not as the scribes" (Matthew 7:29). He can "heal the sick, cleanse the lepers, raise the dead, cast out devils" (Matthew 10:8). Some of his followers even claim that he is "the Christ, the Son of the living God" (Matthew 16:16). In fact, on one occasion he was so brash as to declare, "I am the Son of God" (John 10:36). What would you think? To whom would you go to seek accurate information about this supposedly remarkable man? Would you go to Annas, one-time high priest and head of the Sanhedrin, and ask, "What can you tell me about this Jesus?" Would you go to Pilate, the Roman procurator in Judaea, and ask, "Can you tell me about this new prophet Jesus?" Would you go to Caiaphas, the high priest, Sadducee, and head of the Sanhedrin, and suggest, "This man Jesus appears to have a greater understanding of the law than all of you in the Sanhedrin put together. How do you explain that?" Or would you go to Peter, the Savior's chief apostle, and ask him, "What can you tell me about this Jesus?" Or would you go to Mary Magdalene, the first to see the resurrected Lord, and say, "I understand you are one of Jesus's disciples. Can you tell me about him?" Or would you seek out the man who had been blind from birth and had regained his sight, and ask, "I hear the man called Jesus restored your sight. What can you tell me about him?" If you wanted to know more about Jesus, who would you have asked, had you been there?

Why would anyone feel so strongly about what others believe as to have them put into prison or put to death?

It's understood that most people have a lifetime of thought, energy, and emotion invested in their religious beliefs. Prejudices run deep, and if we're not careful, our passions can get out of control and turn to persecution.

Whenever we ridicule a person's faith or beliefs, whatever they may be, that individual will go on the defensive. Should we expect anything less? Consider this: if anyone were to attack your beliefs, your faith, or your church, saying they were bad, or evil, or wrong, how do you think you would react?

When we attempt to find fault with another person's religion, we do so having made a gross assumption: we assume to know more about his religion than he does. Such an erroneous assumption is of no value whatsoever.

For those who profess to be Christians, all too often their religion is apart from them. Their beliefs are something entirely separate, and it shows in their lifestyle. However, those who are practicing Christians, their religion and their beliefs are an integral part of who they are and cannot be separated from them any more than heat can be separated from fire. The practicing Christian lives his religion. His actions, his deeds, his words, his very thoughts are the fruits of his faith and beliefs (see Matthew 7:16–20).

As you read this work, consider these two statements by the author of the Book of Proverbs: "Only by pride cometh contention" (Proverbs 13:10), and, "He that is of a proud heart stirreth up strife" (Proverbs 28:25).

Pride and contention are constant companions. Contention grows out of prideful power struggles in which we establish ourselves as the protagonist and the other person as our evil antagonist, who must be destroyed if necessary. At the foundation of pride is enmity—enmity toward God and toward our fellow man. Enmity is hatred or ill will.

I feel it's safe to say that all who acknowledge Jesus as the Christ would agree that he is the source of all love, peace, and goodwill. The Lord speaks to us through the Holy Ghost (also referred to as the Holy Spirit, the Spirit of God, or the Spirit) with positive feelings of peace and calm assurance. On the other hand, the devil, Satan, Lucifer, Belial, Beelzebub—whatever you want to call him—is the source of all hatred, contention, and ill will. He speaks to us with negative feelings of contention and anger. So, again, as you read this book, should you experience any rancor, any hostility, any anger, or any ill will, I would ask you to consider the source of such feelings and ask yourself, "Why am I feeling this way? Where are these thoughts coming from?" In the event you do experience any of these negative feelings, I would invite you to put the book down and approach your Heavenly Father in prayer, exercising faith, and ask that He would remove these hostile feelings before continuing to read any further.

As you read, you will see that the topics are, generally speaking, rather broad. They are not itemized and catalogued or in an outline form as they might be in like books. Also, you will see immediately this is not a scholarly work. It was never intended to be. In reality, it's nothing more than a dialogue (albeit one-sided) between you and me. At least that's the approach I took. The presentational style is conversational, at least I hope it is. As in conversation, one idea leads to another. From time to time I will take a side road that will, in due course, lead back to the original topic.

Also, please be aware that when it comes to citing scriptural references from the Bible, I will be using the King James Version. Why? Because the various new translations of the King James Version, with the Revised Standard Version being one example, have been translated by individuals and groups who have questioned the divinity and mission of Jesus Christ. As a result of the translators' doubts and disbeliefs, many passages have been altered to the point as to put into question our Savior's Divine Sonship, along with other basic gospel doctrines.

In the epigraph of this book, I introduced two quotes from the Prophet Isaiah. My goal in presenting this information is two-fold: (1) to set the record straight and (2) apply some "strong reasons," using the Scriptures, in an attempt to explain why Mormons believe the way they do. This is not an attempt to convert; only the Holy Spirit can do that.

WHAT'S WRONG WITH MORMONS?

Close Encounters

*W*hen I reflect back on what was probably my first close encounter with Mormons (it would have been of the third kind), I must have been about five years old. It was summer. I distinctly remember answering a knock at the front door. Looking up, I saw standing there on the front porch two well-scrubbed young men with short hair, dressed in white short-sleeved shirts and ties. Remember, in 1955, all the men and boys wore their hair short, so that was nothing unusual. They asked if either of my parents were home. I went and got Mom. When Mom got to the door and saw those two young men standing there, it was as if all hell had broken loose. You would have thought there were a couple of devils on our front porch, based on her reaction. Although I don't remember so much what Mom said, I clearly remember how she said it. She had a tongue that could clip a hedge. There was no doubt in my tender young mind that she wasn't the least bit happy having these two boys standing on her front porch. Surprised at her reaction, I remember thinking something like, *Wow, why is she so mad at these two guys? They look nice enough.* Now she may have said something to me at the time regarding what had just taken place, but I don't remember it.

My second encounter with Mormons came about the time I was in the ninth grade. There was a nice, quiet family that lived not too far from us. They went to the same church we

1

There was absolutely, positively, no doubt in my mind about how Mom felt about Mormons. In her mind they were a wicked bunch and their teachings were evil. Evidently, according to her, they were something not too far removed from the Prince of Darkness himself. Scary folks, those Mormons!

did. Their surname was McGinn (name has been changed). Their oldest son, also named Jay, and I were in the same classes, both at school and at church. We had pretty much grown up together. All of a sudden, the McGinn family had disappeared, on Sundays anyway. The next time I saw Jay at school I asked him why I hadn't seen him and his family at church. As matter-of-factly and as nonchalantly as any fifteen-year-old would be expected to, he told me they had joined the Mormon Church. For all the impact that piece of information had on me, he may as well have been speaking Chinese.

Chances are—and, again, I really don't remember exactly— I went home and shared with my parents why the McGinns were no longer at church. Just as before, Mom went off on another tirade against Mormons. She made it abundantly clear that there was nothing nice to be said about them, their church, or the McGinns. There was absolutely, positively, no doubt in my mind about how Mom felt about Mormons. In her mind they were a wicked bunch and their teachings were evil. Evidently, according to her, they were something not too far removed from the Prince of Darkness himself. Scary folks, those Mormons!

Now if you've been counting (and there's no reason why you should have been), it was about ten years from my first close encounter to the second. Oddly enough, it would be another ten years before my third close encounter with a Mormon. This time it would take things in a whole new direction, a direction I would have never dreamed of in a million years.

At the time, I was relatively fresh out of college; it had been less than a year, and I was teaching commercial art classes at a high school in Raleigh, North Carolina. Back then, I didn't look any different from the high school students I was teaching. During those first few weeks, I can't tell you how many times I had been stopped in the halls by older, more seasoned teachers asking to see my hall pass. When I told them I was a teacher, some looked suspicious, others looked embarrassed, and still others looked insulted. In any case, part of my responsibilities as a teacher was to help with after-school extracurricular activities. On one such occasion, I was asked to help chaperone and drive a group of students from the theatre classes to Louisburg College to see a performance of a popular pantomime (he had been a protégé of the legendary French mime, Marcel Marceau).

It was a chilly autumn evening, probably a Friday. The air was clear and the wind was cold. We stood outside, shivering in front of the high school, waiting. The kids had divided themselves into their usual cliques and were huddled together to keep warm. I simply wanted to know who was going to be riding in my car. After some boisterous discussion, and even more arm twisting, the students were divided among us adults and were told who they would be riding with. One small excited, animated group, as most theatre students are, came bounding over to my car and announced that it was going to be my privilege to drive them to the performance. I deftly countered that it would indeed be their privilege to ride in my vintage 1961 Mercury Comet.

As I was saying this, my eyes quickly scanned the little group, and I recognized a couple of my own students. Then my gaze came to rest on one particular girl. She was standing behind the others. I hadn't seen her before. Evidently, she was a new student. Looking at her, my eyes lingered for a moment, not because she was such a pretty girl (which she was), but because there seemed to be something different about her. She looked different. It was as though she had an aura around her face. Her countenance was distinctly and discernibly different from all the other students. Brushing it aside, I urged the rowdy bunch into the car, and we hurried on our way.

Over the next several weeks, through school activities, I came to know the girl that rode in my backseat that autumn evening. Her name was Linda. She and her family had just moved to Raleigh from Bellevue, Washington, as the result of her father being transferred by IBM. My first impressions of Linda were correct. She wasn't like most of the other teenagers. She spoke respectfully to the adults. She didn't use profanity or tell dirty jokes. She didn't smoke or drink or do drugs. She dressed stylishly yet modestly. She always had a smile on her face, a kind tone in her voice, and an encouraging word for everyone she spoke to. In short, she was a pleasure to be around. As time passed, I was drawn to Linda. Everyone, it seemed, was drawn to Linda.

At this time I was renting a room from a charming lady by the name of Mary Jane, who lived in a nicer, more affluent section of Raleigh. Mary Jane, a divorced single mom, had a daughter Linda's age, named Laurie, who was one of my art students. Laurie was, in her own way, a sweet girl, but she was the antithesis of Linda in many ways.

One Friday evening, Laurie had a birthday party to which she invited all her friends from school. Even I was invited. (I can't imagine ever inviting one of my high school teachers to a party at my house!) Granted, I lived there, but I pretty much stayed to myself in my downstairs room when family events were in progress. In all fairness, the family, Laurie, her mom, and her older brother did go out of their way to make me feel as though their home was mine. I did feel welcomed there.

Getting back to the birthday party, Linda was among the guests invited. Not only had she been invited, but she had been also asked to spend the night with Laurie. As the night wore on and the party ran down, people began to leave. Later that evening, it was just Laurie and her boyfriend, and Linda and me. I'm not sure where Laurie and her boyfriend were. I think they were upstairs in the kitchen eating the leftovers. Linda and I were sitting cross-legged on the floor in front of the fireplace downstairs in the den, staring into the flames and talking about our innermost thoughts. At one point, I asked Linda if she believed in God. She said she did. I asked her if she was a religious person. She assured me that she was. A few more questions along those lines may have been asked, and then I asked her what church she belonged to. Her answer came, "The Church of Jesus Christ of Latter-day Saints." Everything I had been thinking came to a screeching halt. My first thought was, *That's an awfully long name for a church.* The second thought was, *I have no idea what she's talking about. I've never heard of a church by that name.* Rather than expose my ignorance (after all I was a schoolteacher), I moved on changing the subject to something entirely unrelated.

The next morning, while everyone else was still in bed, I went into the den and pulled the *C* volume of the *World Book Encyclopedia* down from the shelf and looked up "The Church of Jesus Christ of Latter-day Saints." I hadn't gotten past the first sentence of the first paragraph before I learned the awful truth. Linda was a Mormon! The first thought that came to my mind was, *Oh no, I've been fraternizing with the enemy!*

As the weeks progressed, a major disagreement arose between the high school principal and me. To make a long story short, I wound up resigning from my teaching position and found work as a commercial photographer at the pharmaceutical company Burroughs Wellcome (now GlaxoSmithKline).

Shortly after my leaving the school, I was invited to have dinner with Linda and her family at their home. The family consisted of her father (Bill), mother (Marie), older brother (Steve, who was out of the country serving a two-year mission), two younger brothers (Mike and Glen), and the younger twin sisters (Kathy and Karen, or was it Karen and Kathy?). The dinner was excellent. Although I don't remember exactly what was served, I do remember being introduced to a dish that seems to be uniquely Mormon—and that was lime Jell-O with shredded carrots. Actually, it tastes better than it sounds.

I remember thinking as I sat there at the table, listening to their familial banter, *I've never seen a family like this before.* The parents got along with their children, the children got along with their parents, the children got along with each other. Granted, there were times when things got a little out of hand, some of the younger ones got a little rambunctious, and the parents had to step in and exercise some parental control; but, by and large, it was a very calm evening. The unique qualities I had found in Linda, I found in her family. Now having said that, I don't mean to imply that Linda's family was the first nice family I'd ever seen; that simply wouldn't be true. However, there was something different there. There was a warmth and a love in that home that I had never seen before in any home I'd ever been in, including the one where I grew up.

As I was driving home that night, I thought to myself, *Okay, that was a fluke. They were just putting their best foot, or feet, forward. No family that big behaves themselves that well all the time.* As time passed and I drew closer to Linda and her family, I learned that I was mistaken for the most part. Certainly there were times when voices were raised in anger, when doors were slammed in frustration, and when basic human differences butted heads, but invariably these issues were always resolved, in time, in a spirit of love and forgiveness.

As weeks rolled on and the end of the year grew near, Linda had her eighteenth birthday. Because of the respect I had developed for Linda and her family, I asked Bill and Marie, despite of our age difference (I was twenty-four, she had just turned eighteen), if I could take Linda on a date. They agreed.

Our first real date was an Elton John concert. At the time, the rock star was at the height of his career. The long-anticipated concert was being held at the arena in Greensboro, about an hour and a half west of Raleigh. As soon as the tickets became available, I was among the first to buy my two—not the best seats in the house, but we weren't sitting in the nosebleed section either. To make a long story short, I picked up Linda and promised her parents I'd bring her home straight from the concert and that we wouldn't be terribly late. We got to the concert with time to spare and had a wonderful experience. It was, without a doubt, one of the best rock concerts I have ever attended.

That night when we left the arena, it was probably pushing ten thirty, maybe later. As you can imagine, the traffic was a nightmare. It took us what felt like forever to get back to the highway. As we drove home, we talked, we laughed—we had a good time in general. After an hour or so, I noticed that we hadn't seen any signs guiding us back to Raleigh. Somewhere I had gotten turned around. We were headed the wrong way! Not only were we going the wrong way, but we were also lost altogether. The more I tried to get us turned around, the more lost we got.

You have to remember, this was long before the advent of cell phones. We were out in the middle of rural North Carolina, in the middle of the night, without any way of calling Linda's parents and letting them know what had happened. Now I was beginning to feel sick. Linda's dad, Bill, is a huge guy—not fat, mind you—probably six feet six inches tall with the weight to match. Even if he didn't thrash me, I was expecting a major tongue-lashing for keeping his daughter out later than I had promised. I was certain I would never be allowed to date Linda again. Another hour passed. I was on the verge of panicking. Then out of nowhere, we came upon an old gas station. It was closed, of course. Thank heavens there was a phone booth!

Giving Linda some change, she climbed out of the car and called her parents. She was on the phone for what seemed like forever. She explained to them in great detail our misfortune, but I couldn't help wondering what was being said on the other end. Linda came out of the booth smiling. "Everything's fine," she said confidently. "They just said for you to drive carefully." Even though I couldn't believe my ears, it was a relief to hear it.

By the time I finally got Linda home, it must have been around two thirty in the morning. I was sure her folks were waiting at the door. Gathering all my courage, I climbed out of the car, opened the passenger door, and walked Linda up the front steps. She took out her key and unlocked the door. My heart was pounding. She opened the door, and the foyer was empty! There was no Bill standing there with a baseball bat. There was no Marie ready to spring out with a frying pan in hand. I was stunned.

"Where are your folks?" I asked.

"Probably in bed asleep," she replied.

She thanked me for the evening. I apologized for getting us lost. She brushed it aside and went in the house.

Confused, I walked back to the car. *Trust*, I thought. *They actually trust their daughter! Wow! What a concept!*

I didn't see Linda or her parents the next day, a Saturday. I thought it best to lay low even though things appeared to be fine. That Sunday I was invited to dinner. (The condemned man's last meal?) When I arrived, it was as if nothing had happened. I did apologize to her parents, but they assured me that they understood and weren't going to hold it against me. Her mother did say she had something for me. With a broad smile, she handed me an envelope. Bill just sat there with the hint of a smile. Never, in all my years of dating, had a parent ever given me a gift for keeping their daughter out late. Was it a letter bomb? No, it couldn't be that or they wouldn't be seated so close to me. I opened the envelope and pulled out the contents. It was a road map. Evidently, I had a dumbfounded look on my face. Marie, with a twinkle in her eyes and a slight chuckle, said, "Go ahead. Open it."

Unfolding the map, I instantly saw what she had done. "That's in case you ever get lost again," she explained.

Using a highlighting marker, she had drawn a bold circle around Raleigh. Above that, she had printed the word *HOME*.

This was a first. I had committed a major blunder—at least in my mind—and this is how the parents responded. Amazing! In the weeks to come, I would learn a deeper significance to this act, both literally and symbolically, whether it was done wittingly or not.

At this same time I was wrestling with questions and feelings that seemed to be at odds with one another. Constantly there were questions swirling around in my head that could be

I was struggling with low self-esteem and feelings of worthlessness.

classified under three major categories. They were thoughts relating to the questions:

Where did I come from?

Why am I here?

Where am I going after I die?

Along with these questions, I was struggling with low self-esteem and feelings of worthlessness. Life wasn't making any sense to me. It just didn't seem worth living. At the tender age of twenty-four, life seemed to be nothing more than a terrible waste of time.

A couple of weeks later, I was having one of those evenings where life seemed totally pointless. It was a Sunday. I was alone in my room. The lights were out. The door was locked. I sat sprawled in a chrome director's chair, with a black vinyl seat and back, sobbing like a lost little child. I felt terribly alone and horribly afraid. To practically every question of an eternal nature that I had ever asked, the reply was always, "It's a mystery. We're not supposed to know those things. Don't worry about it." But I did worry about it!

One question that weighed on me continually I had asked my mother some fifteen years or so previous to that night. Even today, I can see everything as clearly as if it had happened yesterday. We were in the kitchen. Mom was at the stove fixing dinner. Next to the stove, to the right of it, was a stool. It was one of those old-fashioned step stools, a red-and-white one, with a couple of steps that folded down from under the seat. There I sat, as was often the case, watching Mom cook while we talked about whatever was on my mind. On this particular occasion, I asked her, "What'll happen to us when we die?"

Her reply came instantly, "We'll go to heaven."

"That's not what I mean," I said. "What'll happen to you and me? Will you still be my mom?"

With the confidence that only an adult has and without breaking her stride as she hurried about the little kitchen, she answered, "Oh no, I won't be your mother, and you won't be my son. There's even a chance we won't recognize each other."

Wow! How's a nine-year-old supposed to respond to that? I was crushed. All I could muster was a stunned, "Oh." With that, I slid down off the stool, shuffled upstairs to my bedroom, and collapsed on my bed crying. *She's my mom! How could she forget me? I'm her boy! How could she not recognize me?*

These and like questions were the ones that plagued me that dark night in Raleigh, North Carolina, where I was locked in my darkened room, a box cutter in my right hand, my left arm outstretched, waiting for the blade. It was as if that troubled little boy from the kitchen had returned. After all these years, I hadn't found the answers to our questions. That night, I poured out my heart to God, begging for some answers. I pleaded that He would, somehow, lift me out of that dark hole of despair. I told Him that I simply couldn't go any further. I was tired of living and afraid of dying. Not only that, I lacked the courage to do anything about it.

Laurie's bedroom was across the hall from mine. Even with our doors closed, I could hear the phone ringing. Laurie's bedroom door opened. I saw her shadow at the foot of my door. She was standing there, listening to me cry. There came a tentative knock on my door, and an even more tentative, "Linda's on the phone. She wants to talk to you."

"I don't want to talk to anyone," I barked back.

Laurie disappeared, but not back into her room. A few

moments later, her mother, Mary Jane, banged boldly on the door. "Linda's on the phone!"

I pleaded, "Tell her I can't talk now."

You have to understand, as nice as Mary Jane was, she was never known to pull any punches and she certainly wasn't bashful. With a most authoritative tone she bellowed, "Get your [rear end] out here and answer the [darn] telephone!"

"Fine, tell her I'll be right there." I caught my breath, wiped my eyes, and dragged myself into Laurie's room.

"Hello?"

"Hi, there! How are you doing?" was Linda's bubbly salutation.

"I'm okay." I lied.

"Can you come over? There are a couple of friends here that'd like to meet you."

"Tonight?" I couldn't believe this was happening.

"Yeah, they're here now. You can be here in ten minutes!"

"Okay," I sighed, "I'll be over as quick as I can." I couldn't believe what I was hearing come out of my mouth. As much as I didn't want to be around people, especially on that night, somehow it seemed right to spend some time with Linda and her family. I washed my face, brushed my teeth, tucked in my shirt, and forced myself to climb in the car and drive over to Linda's to meet these two friends of hers.

In front of their house, I dragged myself out of the car and up to their front door. There, I took a deep breath, let it out, and rang the doorbell. The door swung open, and I was greeted by Linda's sparkling eyes and broad disarming smile. Already I was feeling better.

"Come on in! They're downstairs in the family room."

The house was unusually quiet. I couldn't see or hear any of the other family members. Linda took my hand and led me down to the den. There, seated at a game table, were Linda's mother, Marie, and two well-scrubbed young men with short hair, dressed in white short-sleeved shirts and ties. Remember, this was 1974, and hardly any of the men or boys wore their hair short (mine certainly wasn't!), so their haircuts were especially conspicuous. As we entered the room, the two young men politely stood and extended their hands to shake mine. These two fellows, just a few years younger than I was, were introduced to me as missionaries from The Church of Jesus Christ of Latter-day Saints. Unfortunately, with the passage of time, I am ashamed to admit, I have forgotten the names of these two young men. They referred to themselves as Elders. For example, had their last names been Smith and Jones, they would have been introduced as Elder Smith and Elder Jones.

For the next two and a half hours, we talked and got to know one another. For the most part, the conversation was between the Elders and me. Once in a while, Linda or her mother would interject or clarify something that had been said. As we talked, I felt a similar peace with these two young men that I had felt while being with Linda and her family. They were humble and thoughtful and polite. They seemed to care about me and my questions, and more importantly, they had answers. At the end of our first meeting, they asked if we could meet again the following week. I assured them we could. I looked forward to that next meeting.

During the course of our discussion, my mind went back to that first experience I had had some twenty years earlier. There, seated before me, were those two young men that had been standing on our porch, knocking on the front door—Mormon missionaries. The thought came into my mind, *These guys seem nice enough. Why did Mom get so angry?*

During the six weeks I was meeting with the Elders at Linda's home, Christmas arrived. That year it was on a Wednesday. On that particular Christmas, my parents would be visiting my older bother's home in Raleigh. I would go over to his house, and we'd all have our Christmas together. Dad and Mom arrived a few days early. A dinner was planned. I was to come over and bring with me whoever I was dating at the time. For the first time in my life, I wasn't the least bit excited to see my parents, especially my mother. That meant that I would have to introduce Linda to Mom. That meant that Mom would, sooner or later, ask Linda what church she belonged to. That meant Linda would say, "The Church of Jesus Christ of Latter-day Saints." That meant Mom wouldn't need to look it up in the encyclopedia. That meant I was dead meat.

In order to avoid any ugly or embarrassing situations, I took it upon myself to inform Mom and Dad about Linda a day in advance. After spending the better part of that day to gather my courage, I finally told them, "There's something I have to tell you two about Linda. She's a Mormon." Mom flinched imperceptibly, but she didn't explode like I thought she might. Before she could fully comprehend what I had just said, I quickly added, "She's a very sweet girl. Give her a chance before you get any preconceived ideas." She agreed, but it was clear to see that just beneath the surface, she was boiling.

The dinner went very well, actually. Everyone (including Mom) behaved themselves, and Linda was her usual charming self. (Yes, I had warned her.) When I got back from taking Linda home after dinner, I asked Mom what she thought of her. "Was she, a Mormon, as awful as you thought she would be?"

"No, Jay, you were right," she admitted. "She is a sweet a girl. She was well-mannered, she was respectful and polite, fun to be around. But I'm warning you. Be careful. Do not get mixed up with those people."

You would have thought I was playing with dynamite. And what did "those people" mean? It's not like they were lepers. Mom's feelings had me puzzled. Our parents had always raised us boys (there were four of us) to think for ourselves, to exercise the common sense God gave us, not to judge someone before they had a chance to prove themselves, one way or the other. I was at a loss. I simply couldn't understand her attitude toward Mormons. After everything I had seen of Linda and her family, based on the few discussions I had had with the Elders so far, I couldn't help wondering, *What's wrong with Mormons?*

What's wrong with Mormons? That's the question I would like to explore with you throughout the remainder of this book. To do that, I will share with you, as best as I can recall, what the Elders and I had discussed during that six-week period. It may not be in the proper sequence. It will not be verbatim. It will not cover every topic, have every question or every reply; after all, it was over thirty-two years ago. However, it will be totally accurate in content and doctrine.

A Falling Away

*I*n an effort to establish a foundation for everything they were going to teach me, the missionaries introduced me to the concept of the Great Apostasy. This was very important because everything that would follow would stand or fall on the reality of this event.

The reality of a Great Apostasy, or "falling away" as Peter put it, from the true church and its doctrines as instituted by Christ establishes the necessity of a promised restoration. "Where do Mormons come up with these cockamamie ideas? What's wrong with Mormons?"

The first indication of the looming apostasy of the early Christian church—the church Christ established during his mortal ministry—was first mentioned by the Lord himself when he warned his apostles, "Take heed that no man deceive you. For many shall come in my name, saying, I am Christ; and shall deceive many" (Matthew 24:4–5). Then he continues in that same chapter to describe to the apostles the events as they will unfold during and following their apostolic ministry. He speaks of their persecutions and martyrdoms (verse 9); how the local leaders in the various branches of the church shall take offense at each other's teachings and how they will betray one another (verse 10); that many false teachers will establish themselves, not having the proper authority, and deceive many (verse 11); and, as a result of this apostasy, iniquity will be widespread and the

Some of the prophecies predicting the apostasy of the church predate the birth of Christ. The Old Testament prophet Isaiah saw in a vision the condition of the earth at a time of spiritual darkness in which the inhabitants of the earth would be in a general condition of unrighteousness.

love that men are to have one for another (see John 13:34; Matthew 32:29) shall cease (verse 12).

And, indeed, such was the outcome. The evidence of the decline and apostasy of the primitive church, as set up by the Christ, is clearly found in the scriptural record as well as secular history.

Some of the prophecies predicting the apostasy of the church predate the birth of Christ. The Old Testament prophet Isaiah saw in a vision the condition of the earth at a time of spiritual darkness in which the inhabitants of the earth would be in a general condition of unrighteousness. He prophesied, "The earth also is defiled under the inhabitants thereof; because they have transgressed the laws, changed the ordinance, broken the everlasting covenant" (see Isaiah 24:1–6).

Now, some may think this is referencing the violation of the Law of Moses by ancient Israel. But we need to remember, the Law of Moses was never referred to as the "everlasting covenant." The everlasting covenant—the covenant between God and Abraham—preceded the Law of Moses by four hundred and thirty years, and this is discussed in great detail by the Apostle Paul in his Epistle to the Galatians. Therefore, it is clear that Isaiah's prophecy relating to the breaking of the everlasting covenant has no reference to an apostasy from the Mosaic Law, but it refers to a future condition of apostasy following the establishment of the *new* everlasting covenant as established by the Lord during his mortal ministry.

Again, Isaiah records God's lament concerning His apostate children when the Father declared, "Wherefore the Lord said, Forasmuch as this people draw near me with their mouth, and with their lips do honour me, but have removed their heart far from me, and their fear toward me is taught by the precept of men" (Isaiah 29:13). Sounds like a pretty sad state of affairs, doesn't it? However, because of the infinite love and patience our Heavenly Father has for His children, He promised that we would not be left in that miserable state forever. He promised, "Therefore, behold, I will proceed to do a marvellous work among this people, even a marvellous work and a wonder: for the wisdom of their wise men shall perish, and the understanding of their prudent men shall be hid" (Isaiah 29:14). That "marvellous work and a wonder" He spoke of was the restoration of the Gospel in its fullness.

In addition to Isaiah, the Old Testament prophet Amos spoke of this same period when the church of Christ was not to be found upon the earth, when he prophesied, "Behold, the days come, saith the Lord God, that I will send a famine in the land, not a famine of bread, nor thirst for water, but of hearing the word of the Lord; And they shall wander from sea to sea, and from north even to the east, and they shall run to and fro to seek the word of the Lord, and shall not find it" (Amos 8:11–12). It's clear to see from this prophecy that there would be a period in time when the "word of the Lord," the Gospel, would not be found anywhere upon the earth. Men could go from one sea to another, from one point on the compass to another. They could run to and fro, trying to find the true Word of God, but they wouldn't find it.

In the New Testament, the Apostle Paul prophesied of the apostasy that would come prior to the Second Coming when he wrote to the members of the church in Thessalonica: "Let no man deceive you by any means: for that day shall not come, *except there come a falling away first*, and that man of sin be revealed, the son of perdition" (2 Thessalonians 2:3; italics added). Paul warned his missionary companion Timothy of the apostasy when he wrote to him that "the time will come when they will not endure sound doctrine; but . . . they shall turn away their ears from the truth" (2 Timothy 4:3–4).

As recorded by Luke, let's read what the chief apostle, Peter, had to say in these regards: "Repent ye therefore, and be converted, that your sins may be blotted out, when the *times of refreshing* shall come from the presence of the Lord; And he shall send Jesus Christ, which before was preached unto you: Whom the heaven must receive until the *times of restitution of all things*, which God hath spoken by the mouth of all his holy prophets since the world began" (Acts 3:19–21; italics added). This passage, brief as it is, contains some of the most extraordinary information recorded in all the scriptures. Let's examine it in more detail: "when the times of refreshing shall come from the presence of the Lord." The dictionary defines the word *refresh* to mean "to restore strength and animation to life." So it's clear that there was to come a "time of restoring," something that was to come from God's presence. "And he shall send Jesus Christ." Who is "he"? He is God the Father. Whom shall He send? None other than His Only Begotten Son, Jesus Christ, "whom the heaven must receive until the times of restitution of all things."

At the end of the Lord's forty-day ministry after his resurrection, the eleven apostles (remember the traitor Judas had taken his own life) watched as the Savior was received up into heaven (Mark 16:19, Luke 24:52, Acts 1:9), and there he was to stay until "the times of restitution." Going once more to the dictionary, we read the definition of the word *restitution* as being "an act of restoring or a condition of being restored," or putting something back to the way it was originally, to give back or return. This plainly indicates that something had been lost, been forced out of, or was no longer in its original state.

What was to be restored? "All things"! What were these things? These were the things "which God hath spoken by the mouth of all his holy prophets since the world began." These were *all* the things that God had ever revealed to His children through His prophets and His Son, Jesus Christ, even those things the Lord had set up during the course of his mortal ministry—all truth, all law, all commandments, all covenants, all ordinances—that are necessary for the salvation of mankind that will allow us to enter back into the presence of our Father in heaven.

So we see, before the Second Coming of Jesus Christ can take place, his Gospel, which had been lost, had to be restored in its fullness. When was this restoration to take place? Again, we turn to Paul to find the answer, and it is clearly given "that in the dispensation of the fulness of times he might gather together in one *all things* in Christ, both which are in heaven, and which are on earth; even in him" (Ephesians 1:10; italics added).

What exactly is *"the dispensation of the fullness of times"*? First, let's define *dispensation*. A dispensation, as it pertains to the Gospel, is a specific period in which God reveals or dispenses His doctrines to His mortal sons and daughters on earth. One man—a prophet—whom God Himself has selected, prepared, called, and set apart stands at the head of each dispensation. The first, naturally, was Adam. He had the full Gospel in its pure form. He walked and talked with God in the Garden of

Eden before his and Eve's expulsion from the Garden. Each dispensation and the prophet who stood at the head of each is shown as follows:

1. First – Adam
2. Second – Enoch
3. Third – Noah
4. Fourth – Abraham
5. Fifth – Moses
6. Sixth – Peter of the Twelve Apostles

Each dispensation was as unique as the Lord's dealings with His children under those specific circumstances in each period.

Today, we are living in the great and final dispensation. Paul refers to it as "the dispensation of the fullness of times." It is the age when God will "gather together in one all things in Christ, both which are in heaven, and which are on earth" (Ephesians 1:10). Those "things in Christ" are all the doctrines, ordinances, and eternal truths that have ever been taught to man for his eternal salvation; and they are brought together, as promised, in the "restitution of all things," as we have already discussed. This is the time in which the earth and its inhabitants prepare for the Second Coming of our Lord and Savior Jesus Christ. As we have already seen, he cannot return until this restoration takes place!

It's a common belief among all Christian churches that Jesus Christ is the Savior and Redeemer of all mankind. It's also a common belief among those same churches that Jesus did, indeed, establish his church upon the earth, through his personal ministry, during the meridian of time.

Both ecclesiastical history and secular history confirm that a general apostasy developed during and after the apostolic period. Both assert that through this apostasy, the primitive church lost all power and authority as a divine organization. The original and heavenly institution as established by the Christ had, in a very short time, sunken into an earthly organization based upon the philosophies of men mingled with scripture. Many doctrinal truths had been cast aside as acts of political correctness of the time (and it continues today). The sacred ordinances had been changed or done away with altogether. The authority to act in the name of God was gone. The divine light of knowledge and truth no longer shone from heaven; it was nowhere to be found. This period is justly known as the Dark Ages. It was the time prophesied by Isaiah: "Darkness shall cover the earth, and gross darkness the people" (see Isaiah 60:2). The heavens were sealed. Revelations from God were neither received nor recorded.

The church that Jesus had established was totally corrupt. The Albigenses of France recognized this and attempted a reformation of sorts in the thirteenth century. The church leaders considered their attempts heretical and crushed the movement after much cruelty and bloodshed. The next noteworthy revolution came in the fourteenth century, led by Oxford University professor John Wickliffe. He openly attacked the church's leaders for their abusive use of power, denounced the corruption of the church, and boldly pointed out the doctrinal errors that had accumulated over the centuries. The greatest part of Wickliffe's opposition was directed at the church's restrictions on the general population's study of the scriptures. His solution to the problem was to give to the people an English version of the Bible, which he translated from the Vulgate, an early fifth-century version of the Bible.

Elsewhere in Europe, the revolt against the apostate church was being carried out by John Huss and by Jerome of Prague. Both of these religious zealots were martyred as a result of their efforts to return to the truth.

Around the beginning of the sixteenth century, let's narrow

it down to about 1517, the rebellion against the apostate church grew to such proportions as to be referred to as the Reformation. It started in Germany. This movement was led by an Augustinian monk who taught at the University of Wittenburg. His name was Martin Luther. Early in his crusade, Luther's primary complaint dealt with certain practices the church had adopted in the way of buying pardons or forgiveness. These indulgences, as they were called, could even be bought in advance! This was nothing less than selling a license to sin with the promise of absolution before the fact. Being the academic he was, Luther wrote his Ninety-five Theses, railing against this granting of indulgences and other practices, and nailed a copy of it on the front door of the church in Wittenberg. As a result of his questioning these practices of the apostate church, along with the revolt that came about as a result of his writings, the church leaders sent Luther an ultimatum demanding an unconditional recantation of everything he had written or suffer excommunication. Luther was not to be threatened. He burned the letter in public. Shortly thereafter, the leaders made good on their threat, and he was excommunicated from the church. Luther lamented, "I have sought nothing beyond reforming the Church in conformity with the Holy Scriptures. The spiritual powers have been not only corrupted by sin, but absolutely destroyed; so that there is now nothing in them but a depraved reason and a will that is the enemy and opponent of God. I simply say that Christianity has ceased to exist among those who should have preserved it." (*Luther and His Times*, p. 509)

Time and limited space here prevents us from examining in detail what transpired after Luther's excommunication. Suffice it to say, he continued to fight the good fight. Others joined him in his protest movement. The church labeled these protestors as Protestants. The Protestants attempted, with Luther's help, to form an independent church. Martin Luther died in 1546, but the work of reformation continued to grow and spread throughout Europe. Unfortunately, the Protestants had become divided among themselves and broke up into several sects, one contending with the other. This brings to mind an interesting analogy that the missionaries shared with me during those six weeks of intense discussion in Linda's family room.

Imagine, if you will, a large circular glass tabletop. When Jesus established his church, he painted on this glass tabletop the Gospel in its fullness with all its saving truths, ordinances, and covenants. As we examine this table more closely, we see that Christ himself stands as the center post upholding the glass tabletop. We also see there are twelve other legs around the outer edge. These are the twelve apostles. As time passed, the first to be removed was the Lord at his crucifixion. Although the main post had been taken away, the tabletop remained intact because it was being upheld by the remaining apostles that had been set apart by the Lord to that very task. Then, as the apostles died or were martyred, one by one, the remaining legs of the table were removed. With the death of the last apostle, that glass top upon which the Gospel had been painted fell to the ground and shattered into hundreds of pieces. Each of these pieces had upon it a piece of the true church. As men passed by these shards of truth, they picked up a piece here and a piece there and went on their way, forming their own churches. As a result of this, many of the churches have parts of the truth, but no one church has the whole truth in its fullness. As we have seen, God promised that He would once more "gather together in one" all these pieces into a single whole (see Ephesians 1:10).

Getting back to the church's reaction to the reformation, over the next many years the church resorted to barbarous acts of cruelty, mutilation, and even murder in an effort to suppress what it perceived to be a rebellion. What can we say about a church that uses such methods to sustain and support its doctrines? Are persecution and death the means by which truth is to win her battles? How can such a church be the church of Christ?

The reality of the Great Apostasy has been openly accepted by many unbiased theologians and scholars over the centuries. One such nineteenth-century theologian and scholar, William Smith, wrote,

> As God permits men to mar the perfection of his designs in their behalf, and as men have both corrupted the doctrines and broken the unity of the Church, we must not expect to see the Church of Holy Scripture actually existing in its perfection on earth. It is not to be found, thus perfect, either in the collected fragments of Christendom, or still less in any one of these fragments; though it is possible that one of those fragments more than another may approach the scriptural and apostolic ideal which existed only until sin, heresy, and schism, had time sufficiently to develop themselves to do their work. (*Smith's Bible Dictionary*, vol. 1, p. 458)

Smith wasn't alone in his assessment of the apostate condition of the church. Earlier, in the eighteenth century, the Christian theologian John Wesley observed the early decline of spiritual power and the loss of the gifts of the Spirit of God in church and declared,

> It does not appear that these extraordinary gifts of the Holy Spirit were common in the Church for more than two or three centuries. We seldom hear of them after that fatal period when the Emperor

Constantine called himself a Christian, and from a vain imagination of promoting the Christian cause thereby heaped riches and power and honor upon Christians in general, but in particular upon the Christian clergy. From this time they almost totally ceased, very few instances of the kind being found. The cause of this was not, as has been supposed, because there was no more occasion for them, because all the world was become Christians. This is a miserable mistake; not a twentieth part of it was then nominally Christians. The real cause of it was that the love of many, almost all Christians, so-called, was waxed cold. The Christians had no more of the spirit of Christ than the other heathens. The Son of Man, when He came to examine His Church, could hardly find faith upon earth. This was the real cause why the extraordinary gifts of the Holy Ghost were no longer to be found in the Christian church— because the Christians were turned heathens again, and only had a dead form left. (*John Wesley's Works*, Vol. VII, 89:26–27)

The seventeenth-century English theologian and cofounder of the colony Rhode Island, Roger Williams, recognized that the proper authority had also been lost as it pertained to the legal administration of the saving ordinances: "There is no regularly constituted church on the earth, nor any person qualified to administer any church ordinances; nor can there be until new apostles are sent by the great head of the church for who's coming I am seeking" (*Picturesque America, or the Land We Live In*, ed. W. Cullen Bryant, 1872 ed., vol. 1, p. 502).

Statesman, third president of the United States, and avid

student of theology, Thomas Jefferson, also recognized the adulteration of the teachings of the Savior and acknowledged the need for a restoration of the truth when he said,

> The religion builders have so distorted and deformed the doctrines of Jesus, so muffled them in mysticisms, fancies, and falsehoods, have caricatured them into forms so inconceivable, as to shock reasonable thinkers...Happy in the prospect of a restoration of primitive Christianity, I must leave to younger persons to encounter and lop off the false branches which have been engrafted into it by the mythologists of the middle and modern ages" (*Jefferson's Complete Works*, Vol. 7, pp. 210, 257).

These spiritually astute individuals were able to distinguish, under the influence of the Holy Spirit, that the church of Christ established in the meridian of time and the churches that existed in their days were not one and the same. They could clearly see, based on the Bible before them, that the then-existing churches were lacking. These wise, observant men had no agenda, other than seeking after the pure Gospel as it had been delivered originally.

Interestingly enough, as I was preparing for this book, a news article appeared online at MSNBC's site that stated, "Pope Benedict XVI has reasserted the universal primacy of the Roman Catholic Church, approving a document released Tuesday that says Orthodox churches were defective and that other Christian denominations were not true churches." It goes without saying, that declaration offended a great many non-Catholic Christians. Along these same lines, in a pamphlet published ninety years earlier in 1917, the following incident was related by Orson F. Whitney (a latter-day apostle):

Many years ago a learned man, a member of the Roman Catholic Church, came to Utah and spoke from the stand of the Salt Lake Tabernacle. I became well-acquainted with him, and we conversed freely and frankly. A great scholar, with perhaps a dozen languages at his tongue's end, he seemed to know all about theology, law, literature, science and philosophy. One day he said to me: "You Mormons are all ignoramuses. You don't even know the strength of your own position. It is so strong that there is only one other tenable in the whole Christian world, and that is the position of the Catholic Church. The issue is between Catholicism and Mormonism. If we are right, you are wrong; if you are right, we are wrong; and that's all there is to it. The Protestants haven't a leg to stand on. For if we are wrong, they are wrong with us since they were a part of us and went out from us while if we are right, they are apostates whom we cut off long ago. If we have the apostolic succession from St. Peter, as we claim, there is no need of Joseph Smith and Mormonism; but if we have not that succession, then such a man as Joseph Smith was necessary, and Mormonism's attitude is the only consistent one. It is either the perpetuation of the gospel from ancient times, or the restoration of the gospel in latter days." (LeGrand Richards, *A Marvelous Work and a Wonder*, Deseret Book Co., 1976, p. 3)

The Catholic gentleman brings up an interesting point. Paul's first Epistle to the church in Corinth shows there were already serious divisions among Christians at that time.

Some boasted they were of Paul, others of Apollos, others of Cephas, and still others of Christ, which led Paul to ask, "Is Christ divided?" (1 Corinthians 1:13). This ongoing strife among the new Christians caused Paul to criticize them for being carnally minded (see 1 Corinthians 3:3–4). He had admonished them, "By the name of our Lord Jesus Christ, [see] that ye all speak the same thing, and that there be no divisions among you; but that ye be perfectly joined together in the same mind and the same judgment" (1 Corinthians 1:10).

So if Christ is not divided, then we must ask ourselves: Are all the churches on earth true? Is there more than one Gospel? Is there more than one plan of salvation? The answers are obvious! There cannot be more than one true church. There cannot be more than one Gospel. There is only one plan of salvation. With so many churches, how can today's Christians "be perfectly joined together"? With so much division among Christians, how can they "all speak the same thing"? With so many conflicting doctrinal teachings among Christians, how can they have "the same mind and the same judgment"? This being the case, and since Christ is not divided, then the existence of these conflicting Christian churches is proof positive of the Great Apostasy.

As we have plainly seen, the Great Apostasy was real. There was indeed, just as it was prophesied and recorded in the Bible, a "falling away." It cannot be denied any more than the Holocaust. With the advent of the Dispensation of the Fullness of Times, the appointed time had arrived for the "times of refreshing." The "times of restitution of all things" was at hand, and God's hand cannot be stayed!

Mouthpiece of the Lord

*T*o briefly recap the timeline, Jesus was born, grew to adulthood, called twelve apostles, established his church, atoned for the sins of mankind, and was resurrected. After the apostles died, and within one to two hundred years, the church was in a state of total apostasy. The heavens were sealed; there were no revelations because there were no prophets to receive them. The earth was in total spiritual darkness. Now it's the Dispensation of the Fullness of Times. The time has come for the restitution of all things, as was promised by prophets and apostles. The only problem is there are no prophets on the earth to receive these "things." What's God to do?

Early on in my discussions with the missionaries, one of the questions I brought up almost immediately was, "If there were prophets anciently, why aren't there prophets now?"

In perfect unison the Elders replied, "There are!"

But today, the uninformed cry, "The heavens are sealed. God no longer has need to speak to mankind! What's wrong with Mormons?" But I ask, how can anyone who follows the teachings of the Bible believe otherwise?

When I heard that there were prophets on the earth today, I felt a calm relief wash over me as I thought, *It only stands to reason.*

As we saw in chapter 2, God had raised a specific prophet to

In each dispensation, when the people had wandered away from the true faith in God, it was the prophet's duty to restore that faith and remove the false views...

stand at the head of each dispensation. Again, they were

1. Adam
2. Enoch
3. Noah
4. Abraham
5. Moses
6. Peter of the Twelve Apostles

Between each of these heads of each dispensation, the Lord also raised up subsequent prophets to carry out his work. Some examples would be Isaac, Jacob, Joshua, Samuel, Elijah, Isaiah, Jeremiah, Daniel, Amos, and Malachi from the Old Testament. From the New Testament we have examples in John the Baptist, Matthew, Mark, Luke, John, Paul, and James.

It is the work of a prophet to act as God's mouthpiece on earth, to make known His mind and His will to His children. Anciently, prophets testified to men of God's character and attributes. They also had the unenviable responsibility to denounce sin and foretell its punishments if those guilty of such behavior didn't repent and turn back to God. Therefore, a prophet, above all else, is a preacher of righteousness.

In each dispensation, when the people had wandered away from the true faith in God, it was the prophet's duty to restore that faith and remove the false views that had arisen about the character of God and the nature of the divine requirements placed upon the sons and daughters of the Eternal Father.

Prior to the birth of Jesus Christ, those prophets who spoke of his coming spoke of future events. Their words were *Messianic prophecies*. Those who have spoken since the Messiah's mortal ministry have spoken of past events. Their words are *Messianic testimonies*. Down from the days of Adam until now, prophets have taught salvation is to be had only through Jesus Christ (see John 14:6).

God, the Eternal Father, is the same yesterday, today, and forever, isn't He? His truths, covenants, and doctrines are absolute. If He were changeable and unpredictable as man is, He would, by the very nature of things, cease to be God, wouldn't you agree? "God is not the author of confusion" (1 Corinthians 14:33), Paul reminded the wayward saints in the wicked city of Corinth. In the Epistle of James, that apostle declared that "the Father of lights" is one "with whom is no variableness, neither shadow of turning" (James 1:17). Paul taught the Hebrews that "it was impossible for God to lie" (Hebrews 6:18). Moses, who led Israel out of Egypt, made it abundantly clear that "God is not a man, that he should lie; neither the son of man, that he should repent: hath he said, and shall he not do it? or hath he spoken, and shall he not make it good?" (Numbers 23:19). The Apostle Peter taught Cornelius, a Roman centurion, "of a truth I perceive that God is no respecter of persons" (Acts 10:34).

Therefore, if God is the same always and never changing, if He is no respecter of persons, if salvation is only through true and correct principles as given by Him through Jesus Christ, then everyone, regardless of the time in which they lived—past, present, or future—are deserving of the saving ordinances of the Gospel. All are deserving of knowing the mind and will of their Eternal Father. If those of times past were deserving of having God speak to them, then we, today, are just as deserving, aren't we?

Hence, with the reality of the Great Apostasy, it stands to reason there needs to be a restoration as we have seen. Since there needs to be a restoration, it stands to reason, as indicated in times past, that a prophet must be set up before the people to act as God's mouthpiece to carry out the task of delivering His message(s).

Teaching the necessity of prophets and continuing revelation is at the heart of the persecution and the outrage against The Church of Jesus Christ of Latter-day Saints. "Which of the prophets have not your fathers persecuted? and they have slain them which shewed before of the coming of the Just One; of whom ye have been now the betrayers and murderers" (Acts 7:52), asked Stephen of those who stoned him to death. Such is the method of those whose hearts are hardened against the truth. Why is this the case? Why do God's children reject and destroy the very ones whom He has sent to show them the way back to His presence?

Just as there is opposition in all things, such as hot and cold, black and white, hard and soft, wet and dry, light and dark, virtue and vice, so there is an opposite to Jesus Christ— that is the devil, known as Lucifer (see Isaiah 14:12). He stands as direct opposition to all things in Christ. Prophets teach that salvation is in Christ and correct doctrine. Where prophets are, there is salvation also. Is it any wonder, then, that Lucifer fights the prophets at every turn and seeks their destruction?

The sad irony to this is, more often than not, this persecution is heaped upon the prophets, and those who follow them, by those who are or consider themselves to be religiously inclined. Again, we can confirm this by the Bible itself. Jesus Christ lamented, "O Jerusalem, Jerusalem, which killest the prophets, and stonest them that are sent unto thee" (Luke 13:34). These were the religious leaders of the time to whom the Lord was speaking. Such was the case prior to his first coming: "But they mocked the messengers of God, and despised his words, and misused his prophets" (2 Chronicles 36:16). "For the children of Israel have forsaken thy covenant, thrown down thine altars, and slain thy prophets with the sword; and I, even I only, am left; and they seek my life, to take it away" (1 Kings 19:10) was the prophet Elijah's reply to God when asked why he was hiding in a cave. The Apostle Paul was taken to Rome and martyred for his teachings. Peter, the chief apostle, also died a martyr's death. (See also Hebrews 11:32–37.) And can we forget the Chief Prophet himself, who was slain for the sins of world because of what he taught?

Persecution, in all its forms, comes from the devil. Those who persecute the prophets think they are doing God a favor. Jesus declared this very fact to his apostles, "Yea, the time cometh, that whosoever killeth you will think that he doeth God service" (John 16:2). Be that as it may, through the prophet Isaiah, God has promised that His work will go forth: "No weapon that is formed against thee shall prosper; and every tongue that shall rise against thee in judgment thou shalt condemn. This is the heritage of the servants of the Lord, and their righteousness is of me, saith the Lord" (Isaiah 54:17). Such is the testimony of history.

With this thought in mind, I would like to discuss the need, if there is one, for prophets. Exercising some basic reasoning and considering the condition of the world today, considering the deterioration of the family, considering the demise of moral standards and values, considering the cruelty people are heaping upon one another, considering the state of government, considering all the chaos in and amongst the nations, wouldn't you agree that now, more than any time in the history of the world, we need the voice of God to direct us?

In a court of law, it is not unusual for attorneys to meet and discuss each other's side of the argument to determine if they can find some common ground in order to save time and effort.

As I mentioned in the preface, since you're reading this book, I will assume that you are a Christian. It is assumed that you believe in the Bible, that being the Old and New Testaments. It is also assumed that you believe in prayer. There is our common ground. But if I were to ask you if God speaks to men today, you would, more than likely, say, "No, the heavens are sealed." Now we are no longer standing on common ground. But wait…

Has God at any time in the history of the world spoken to men? Of course he has! Both the Old and New Testaments are evidence of such occurrences. For example, He spoke to Adam, He spoke to Noah, He spoke to Abraham, He spoke to Moses, He spoke to Joshua, and all the other prophets. Okay, now we're back on common ground.

Assuming that you are a Christian, it is supposed that you believe that Jesus of Nazareth was the Son of God. After the death and resurrection of Jesus Christ, can you think of any occasion when God spoke to anyone? "Well," you say, "there was the time Saul was on his way to Damascus. He heard a voice from heaven." And whose voice was that? The speaker addressing Saul identified himself as Jesus Christ, did he not? (See Acts 9.) So we can see that even after the death of Jesus Christ, God continued to talk to men on earth. Can you think of any other examples? How about when God spoke to Peter and commanded him to take the Gospel to the Gentiles? (See Acts 10.) Then there was the time the Lord appeared to Paul giving him comfort. (See Act 23.) And what about the vision that God revealed to John while on the Isle of Patmos? (See Revelation.) It's clear to see that it was standard operating procedure for God to speak to men in biblical times.

Now some of the more studious readers may say that such communication stopped somewhere around the end of the first century. That is indeed true, just as we saw in the previous chapter. However, some of you may not accept that. So let me ask you, Why do you think God would stop communicating with His children?

If I were to suggest that He had lost the power to do so, you would, more than likely, accuse me of blasphemy. All right, if He still has the power to speak to His children, maybe He doesn't speak to us because He doesn't love us and He doesn't care what happens to us anymore. That doesn't work either because we know that "God so loved the world that He gave His only begotten Son" (John 3:16). And we also know that He is no respecter of persons (Acts 10:34).

Where does that leave us? We know He can speak to us. We know He does love us. So there's only one other viable answer: we don't need Him. Since the death of Christ, mankind has, in all its endeavors, advanced so far and so completely that we simply don't need God anymore. Would you agree with that? Neither would I. There is nothing lacking on God's part. God does speak to men today, but it requires faith on their part to hear Him.

I would say today, more than any other time in the history of the world, we need prophets to guide us and direct us through these perilous times in order that we may prepare ourselves to be worthy to receive Christ at his Second Coming.

It is self-evident from the scriptures that, from Adam to John the Revelator, God directed the affairs of His children by personal communication through His commissioned servants, the prophets.

Addressing the saints in Galatia, the Apostle Paul, whose calling was "not of men, neither by man, *but by Jesus Christ, and God the Father,* who raised him from the dead" (Galatians 1:1; italics added), testified in his Epistle, "For I neither received it of man, neither was I taught it, but by the revelation of Jesus Christ" (Galatians 1:12). The *it* he is referring to is his testimony of the truthfulness of the Gospel of Jesus Christ. He received a witness that the Gospel and its doctrines are not from any man or men, but they were revealed to him in their fullness by none other than the Lord himself. The Lord spoke directly to him. This is known as *revelation.* Revelation is the means by which God makes known to men divine truths, whatever they may be.

Through revelation, the Lord reveals the "mysteries of the kingdom" (see Matthew 13:11; Luke 8:10) to his servants. Knowing as we do that the Lord is unchangeable, does it make any sense that a just God would bless his children in one dispensation with current revelation of His will while in another leave His children to struggle as best they can according to the laws of a former time?

"Okay, what about the period of apostasy?" Good question! We need to remember, God didn't take away the Gospel. Men, by their own doing, adulterated the Gospel by choice as a result of their own wickedness. Jesus spoke about salt losing its savor, stating that once this has happened, it is "good for nothing, but to be cast out, and to be trodden under foot of men" (Matthew 5:13). First of all, salt cannot lose its savor, or saltiness. In order for that to happen, the measure of salt has to become diluted with some other substance, like sand for example. It wasn't uncommon at the time of Christ for this very thing to happen, and when it did, the salt was "good for nothing," or it was no longer of any value for its purpose of adding savor to food. As a result, it was thrown out onto the ground "to be trodden under the feet of men." Such was the case with the Gospel shortly after the deaths of the apostles. The Gospel had become so polluted with the philosophies of men, it was no longer pure. It was no longer fit for its intended purpose. As a result of this wickedness, this adulteration of the Gospel, God allowed men to suffer the consequences of their actions for a season. The Lord's program is unchangeable. His laws are immutable.

Revelation is essential to the restoration of the Lord's church. If there were no revelation—the knowledge of God's will—there wouldn't be the proper doctrines, covenants, and ordinances that comprise the Gospel. If there were no revelations, there couldn't be the proper callings and ordinations of His ministers by which the Gospel is to be administered. How could any such minister ever expect to teach the mind and will of God if he believed the heavens were sealed? How could he carry out the Lord's work if he claimed there were no such things as visions or revelations and that all such things had ceased with the apostles, and that there wouldn't be any more revelations? Based on everything we've seen thus far in the scriptures, it stands to reason that he couldn't!

The Dispensation of the Fullness of Times had arrived. God was about to put His hand to work one last time, as He had promised, in the restitution of all things. In order to accomplish this, He would need to call forth a prophet—one individual He would select to stand at the head of this final dispensation, prior to His Son's Second Coming, just as He had done in past dispensations. That individual would be a farm boy with little formal education who lived in a small, obscure town in upstate New York. His name was Joseph Smith Jr.

The year was 1820. There were great debates with much

religious controversy in the area where Joseph lived. In his own words,

> There was in the place where we lived [Manchester] an unusual excitement on the subject of religion. It commenced with the Methodists, but soon became general among all the sects in that region of country. Indeed, the whole district of country seemed affected by it, and great multitudes united themselves to the different religious parties, which created no small stir and division amongst the people, some crying, "Lo, here! and others, Lo, there!" Some were contending for the Methodist faith, some for the Presbyterian, and some for the Baptist. (Joseph Smith—History [JSH] 1:5)

All the religious controversy was confusing to him. It was at this point in my discussions with the Elders that I, personally, could easily identify with what Joseph had experienced. In the area where I grew up, there were several denominations of churches. Some of those same denominations had two or more congregations within the same area, and no two taught the same doctrines or interpreted the scriptures in the same way! Again, quoting the boy Joseph, "But so great were the confusion and strife among the different denominations, that it was impossible for a person young as I was, and so unacquainted with men and things, to come to any certain conclusion who was right and who was wrong" (JSH 1:8).

I know how he felt. But why should this surprise us? The world, which included upstate New York, was deep in apostasy. Joseph continues,

> In the midst of this war of words and tumult of opinions, I often said to myself: What is to be done?

Who of all these parties are right; or, are they all wrong together? If any one of them be right, which is it, and how shall I know it?

While I was laboring under the extreme difficulties caused by the contests of these parties of religionists, I was one day reading the Epistle of James, first chapter and fifth verse, which reads: "If any of you lack wisdom, let him ask of God, that giveth to all men liberally, and upbraideth not; and it shall be given him."

Never did any passage of scripture come with more power to the heart of man than this did at this time to mine. It seemed to enter with great force into every feeling of my heart. I reflected on it again and again, knowing that if any person needed wisdom from God, I did; for how to act I did not know, and unless I could get more wisdom than I then had, I would never know; for the teachers of religion of the different sects understood the same passages of scripture so differently as to destroy all confidence in settling the question by an appeal to the Bible. (JSH 1:10–12)

The naïve fourteen-year-old boy Joseph took James at his word. He decided he would indeed "ask of God," and he did this, obviously, having the faith that God would reply to his honest petition. Finding a quiet, solitary place in a grove of trees not too far from his father's farm, he was ready to seek his answer. However, as we would say today, "He got more than he bargained for!"

After I had retired to the place where I had previously designed to go, having looked around me, and finding myself alone, I kneeled down and began to offer up the desires of my heart to God. I had scarcely done so, when immediately I was seized upon by some power which entirely overcame me, and had such an astonishing influence over me as to bind my tongue so that I could not speak. Thick darkness gathered around me, and it seemed to me for a time as if I were doomed to sudden destruction.

But, exerting all my powers to call upon God to deliver me out of the power of this enemy which had seized upon me, and at the very moment when I was ready to sink into despair and abandon myself to destruction—not to an imaginary ruin, but to the power of some actual being from the unseen world, who had such marvelous power as I had never before felt in any being—just at this moment of great alarm, I saw a pillar of light exactly over my head, above the brightness of the sun, which descended gradually until it fell upon me.

It no sooner appeared than I found myself delivered from the enemy which held me bound. When the light rested upon me I saw two Personages, whose brightness and glory defy all description, standing above me in the air. One of them spake unto me, calling me by name and said, pointing to the other—*This is My Beloved Son. Hear Him!*

My object in going to inquire of the Lord was to know which of all the sects was right, that I might know which to join. No sooner, therefore, did I get possession of myself, so as to be able to speak, than I asked the Personages who stood above me in the light, which of all the sects was right (for at this time it had never entered into my heart that all were wrong)—and which I should join.

I was answered that I must join none of them, for they were all wrong; and the Personage who addressed me said that all their creeds were an abomination in his sight; that those professors were all corrupt; that: "they draw near to me with their lips, but their hearts are far from me, they teach for doctrines the commandments of men, having a form of godliness, but they deny the power thereof."

He again forbade me to join with any of them; and many other things did he say unto me, which I cannot write at this time. When I came to myself again, I found myself lying on my back, looking up into heaven. When the light had departed, I had no strength; but soon recovering in some degree, I went home. (JSH 1:15–20; italics in the original)

Sounds too fantastic, doesn't it? It might even make you angry. You wonder, "What's wrong with Mormons?" (If you haven't read the preface of this book, *please* go back and do so now!)

Okay, let's consider a couple of things before we move on here. First, every Christian religion that existed at that time (and all but one that exists today), and certainly every one that Joseph was exposed to, taught that God was without body, parts, or passions. He was one God carrying out three duties as one—God the Father, God the Son, and God the Holy Ghost—the Holy Trinity. It's as if one being were wearing three hats, depending on the job he was fulfilling at any given moment. But there in that grove the boy saw "two Personages"! The one, God the Father, "pointed to the other," God the Son (Jesus Christ), and acknowledged him as "My Beloved Son."

Where did the boy Joseph get such an idea when such an idea didn't exist? Had he been making it up based upon his knowledge at the time, wouldn't he have said God (alone) appeared to me, instead of saying "two Personages" appeared to me?

When and where did the idea of three-in-one come into being as it pertains to the "mystery of the trinity"? Actually, it came about as a by-product of the Great Apostasy. There was a conflict between the speculative Greek philosophy and the literal understanding of the earliest Christians that produced contentions, which were threatening to widen the political divisions in the rapidly fragmenting Roman Empire. In an effort to mend this widening rift, Emperor Constantine convened the first churchwide council in AD 325 in an attempt to end the various disagreements and arguments regarding the Godhead, which were prevalent at the time. So under the direction of temporal politics, the nature of God was established by apostate churchmen, philosophers, and ecclesiastical leaders. The document that contained their compromise came to be known as the Nicene Creed. Some years later, another council was held in these same regards and they followed up with the Athanasian Creed, which in part stated,

> The Father incomprehensible, the Son incomprehensible, and the Holy Ghost incomprehensible. The Father eternal, the Son eternal, and the Holy Ghost eternal. And yet there are not three eternals, but one eternal. As also there are not three incomprehensibles, nor three uncreated; but one uncreated, and one incomprehensible. So likewise the Father is Almighty, the Son Almighty, and the Holy Ghost Almighty; and yet there are not three Almighties, but one Almighty. So the Father is God, the Son is

God and the Holy Ghost is God, and yet there are
not three Gods but one God.

Today, as then, to one degree or another, the churches continue to argue the nature of God, that is all churches but one.

The true nature of God was the first newly revealed truth,
and that's what makes this unique event so exciting. God, the
Eternal Father, had revealed Himself *and* His Son to the prophet-
to-be. Remember, one of the duties of a prophet is to *testify to
men of God's character and attributes.* We'll talk more about this
later in greater detail.

The second revealed truth that makes this so exceptional is
that it was the Son, Jesus Christ, who declared that the churches
"were all wrong," not Joseph, and "that all their creeds were
an abomination" in his sight. After all, it was he, Christ—the
Son—who established his church under his Father's direction
(see John 4:34; 6:38; 8:28; 9:4). Remember, salvation comes
through Christ; therefore, in light of the falling away—the
apostasy—from his church that existed at that time, it makes
perfect sense that he would say, "They draw near to me with their
lips, but their hearts are far from me, they teach for doctrines the
commandments of men, having a form of godliness, but they
deny the power thereof." Why should such a declaration from
the Savior make anyone angry? Wouldn't you think that when
God fulfills His promises to restore the Gospel in its fullness
and that when certain prophecies come to pass that those who
profess to be followers of Christ would rejoice and shout for
joy? But they neither rejoiced nor shouted for joy (and many
don't today). Instead, they went back to that devil-inspired
persecution.

The boy Joseph experienced this:

I soon found...that my telling the story had excited

a great deal of prejudice against me among professors of religion, and was the cause of great persecution, which continued to increase; and though I was an obscure boy, only between fourteen and fifteen years of age, and my circumstances in life such as to make a boy of no consequence in the world, yet men of high standing would take notice sufficient to excite the public mind against me, and create a bitter persecution; and this was common among all the sects—all united to persecute me. (JSH 1:22)

He describes one experience he had in the company of one of the local ministers: "I took occasion to give him an account of the vision which I had had. I was greatly surprised at his behavior; he treated my communication not only lightly, but with great contempt, saying it was all of the devil, that there were no such things as visions or revelations in these days; that all such things had ceased with the apostles, and that there would never be any more of them." (JSH 1:21).

How audacious! Who is justified in closing the mouth of God? Where is the logic in thinking that God is a respecter of persons, who no longer loves His children as He did anciently; that He is a God who doesn't keep His promises; that He is a God who changes and who isn't consistent from one generation to the next?

Changing gears ever so slightly, speaking of Joseph Smith, let's consider the following: although it's not proof in and of itself of his divine calling as Prophet of the Dispensation of the Fullness of Times, let's take into account what Joseph accomplished in just translating the Book of Mormon alone. The book was translated, dictated, written—however you want to describe it—in just a little over two months. Do you know

MOUTHPIECE OF THE LORD

anyone who could write a book that is nearly six hundred pages in two months? In addition to the mere six hundred pages, the book would have to contain fifty-four chapters dealing with wars, twenty-one historical chapters, fifty-five chapters on visions and prophecies (remember, on top of that those visions and prophecies must agree with the Bible). The book would require seventy-one chapters on doctrine and exhortation, and here too he must make certain that every statement is consistent with the Bible. The book must also contain twenty-one chapters on the ministry of Christ; and everything written claiming to be said by Jesus, everything he did, and every testimony given by him must correspond completely with the New Testament. In addition to all that, the writer would need to devise figures of speech, similes, metaphors, narration, exposition, description, oratory, epic, lyric, logic, and parables throughout the storytelling. Who do you know that would be willing to take on such a Herculean challenge with a little over two months in which to complete it?

Many of those who have attempted to discredit Joseph Smith have attempted to describe various methods as to how the Book of Mormon was translated. The fact of the matter is we don't exactly know how he did it. Joseph never explained the method he used in the translating. Once, his brother Hyrum, during a conference meeting in Ohio, called on Joseph to explain how the work of translation was done. Joseph responded by saying, "It was not intended to tell the world all the particulars of the coming forth of the book of Mormon," and that "it was not expedient for him to relate these things" (*History of the Church*, 7 vols, 1, p. 237).

Based on certain scriptural accounts we do know, speaking very broadly, that Joseph had to have the spirit of revelation. In explaining this concept to Oliver Cowdery, Joseph's scribe during the translation process, the Lord explained,

> Verily, verily, I say unto you, that assuredly as the Lord liveth, who is your God and your Redeemer, even so surely shall you receive a knowledge of whatsoever things you shall ask in faith, with an honest heart, believing that you shall receive a knowledge concerning the engravings of old records, which are ancient, which contain those parts of my scripture of which has been spoken by the manifestation of my Spirit.
>
> Yea, behold, I will tell you in your mind and in your heart, by the Holy Ghost, which shall come upon you and which shall dwell in your heart.
>
> Now, behold, this is the spirit of revelation. (Doctrine and Covenants 8:1–3)

The Lord also provided the physical means, the Urim and Thummim, to aid the translation "and gave him [Joseph] power from on high, by the means which were before prepared, to translate the Book of Mormon" (Doctrine and Covenants 20:8). "Now, behold, I say unto you [Joseph], that because you delivered up those writings which you had power given unto you to translate by the means of the Urim and Thummim, into the hands of a wicked man, you have lost them" (Doctrine and Covenants 10:1).

You're probably wondering, "What is a Urim and Thummim?" The Urim and Thummim was made of two stones called seer stones or interpreters. The Hebrew words *urim* and *thummim* are both plural, meaning "lights" and "perfections." Ordinarily they are carried in a breastplate over the heart. (Exodus 28:30; Leviticus 8:8). They are aids in receiving revelations and in translating ancient records written in a foreign language. Aaron and the priests in Israel had them from generation to generation. (See Exodus 28:30; Leviticus 8:8; Numbers 27:21; Deuteronomy 33:8; 1 Samuel 28:6; Ezra 2:63; Nehemiah 7:65.)

The gift of translation that had been given to Joseph was dependent upon his obedience to the Lord's direction. As a result of disobedience, Joseph lost that gift for a while until he had repented for his disobedience:

"And you also lost your gift at the same time, and your mind became darkened.

"Nevertheless, it is now restored unto you again; therefore see that you are faithful and continue on unto the finishing of the remainder of the work of translation as you have begun" (Doctrine and Covenants 10:2–3).

If anyone, regardless of what church he belongs to, tries to give you specific information on the method of translation of the Book of Mormon, you can rest assured that (1) he does not know what he's talking about, and (2) he is providing you with false and erroneous information.

So, based on everything we've seen, it's clear that God is never changing. He is the same yesterday, today, and forever. He does indeed keep His promises. There was indeed a falling away. The Great Apostasy happened. God raised up a prophet to stand at the head of the last dispensation, that being the Dispensation of the Fullness of Times, just as He had done in times past. With a prophet called, the restitution of all things could begin. The Gospel of Jesus Christ could be restored in its fullness. In order to do that, the Lord will have to reveal his mind and will to the prophet, along with all the lost truths, covenants, ordinances, and doctrines that enable men to return to the presence of their Father in heaven.

There is a living prophet today who, under the direction of Jesus Christ, continues to direct the affairs of the Church. The

WHAT'S WRONG WITH MORMONS?

prophet is known as the president of The Church of Jesus Christ of Latter-day Saints. He is the authorized successor to Joseph Smith. He along with his two counselors comprises the First Presidency (a similitude of the Godhead as were Peter, James, and John). They and the present twelve apostles can trace their authority directly to Jesus Christ in an unbroken chain of priesthood ordinations.

The Godhead

One of the most offensive doctrines of The Church of Jesus Christ of Latter-day Saints, according to other Christians, is the doctrine that states God the Father (Elohim), God the Son (Jesus Christ, known prior to his birth as Jehovah), and God the Holy Ghost (also known as the Holy Spirit) are three distinct, separate, individual beings. The first two having bodies of flesh and bone with the third being a Spirit Personage (without a tangible body). "How could they possibly believe such a thing? What's wrong with Mormons?"

These three glorious individuals—God the Father, God the Son, and God the Holy Ghost—make up the Godhead or governing body of all creation. They share the same character, attributes, and perfections. They are unified in all things and have all power. They are one in all things. Paul stated that in Christ "dwelleth all the fullness of the Godhead bodily" (Colossians 2:9). That's to say, in Christ is found the same justice and judgment, the same mercy and grace, and the same power of the other members of the Godhead (see Hebrew 1:1–3). Because of their unity, they are spoken of as being one—one Godhead or presiding authority.

The faith of the members of The Church of Jesus Christ of Latter-day Saints centers in Jesus Christ, and through that faith in him, they have faith in God the Father and the Holy Ghost, who is their minister. Their beings are as separate as are their roles. Those roles, broadly speaking, are

1. God the Creator
2. God the Redeemer
3. God the Testator

Each role is an individual part of one plan—the plan of salvation. Now let's take a closer look at each member and his responsibility.

The first member of the Godhead is *God the Father*. He is the one supreme God. He is the Father of our spirits. It is to Him and Him only that we pray, in the name of Jesus Christ. We are His sons and daughters in the literal and full meaning of the word. We are His spirit children. Paul, admonishing the Hebrew saints, taught, "We have had fathers of our flesh which corrected us, and we gave them reverence: shall we not much rather be in subjection unto the Father of spirits, and live?" (Hebrews 12:9) The resurrected Lord speaking to Mary Magdalene said, "I ascend unto my Father, and your Father" (John 20:17), attesting that God both has a Son in mortality and that He is the Father of all mankind. All of ancient Israel prayed, "O God, the God of the spirits of all flesh" (Numbers 16:22). And Jesus taught the people to pray, "Our Father which art in heaven" (Matthew 6:9). How plainly can the scriptures teach us of our relationship to our God, the Father of all?

God the Father, by the nature of that great calling/title, is also *God the Creator*. He is, in every sense of the word, the Creator of "all things that are" (Acts 14:15). He is the source of all creative power. "But wait," you say, "John 1:1–3 states that 'all things' were made by Jesus, 'the Word.'" That's true! The Father, as has been pointed out, is the source of all creative power, and as such He was able to delegate that power to His Son. The Son himself declared that he is not self-regulating or independent of the Father: "I do nothing of myself" (John 8:28; see John 5:19, 30). There were two major creative actions that God the Father alone was responsible for: the creation of our spirits, including that of Jesus, and the creation of the bodies for Adam and Eve. Comparing the construction of a skyscraper to the creation of the earth as an analogy, imagine the Father as the chief architect and contractor. Now imagine Jesus as the subcontractor on site who carries out the actual construction.

God the Father is also *God the Author* of the plan of salvation. It couldn't be any other way. He, and He alone, was in the position to ordain (organize) laws and establish the system whereby His children, including Jesus, could be saved. Again, He may delegate others to carry out certain tasks in the plan, but only He could lay out the specifics and determine how salvation was to be obtained. As to His high and glorious rank as an exalted man (this is another doctrine that really ruffles the feathers of other Christians), the plan of salvation becomes wondrously clear and many of the so-called mysteries become more easily understood.

At this point, regarding godhood, let me simply quote our Lord and Savior Jesus Christ. He left us all with the divine injunction: "Be ye therefore perfect, even as your Father which is in heaven is perfect" (Matthew 5:48). The King James Version of the Bible was translated from the Greek. The Greek word translated as *perfect* means "complete, finished, fully developed." Isn't this the charge a father would give his children? If perfection were to be realized in the form of a nebulous spirit, then why will our bodies be resurrected?

On one particular Sabbath, the Lord had plucked an ear of corn because he was hungry. Some of the members of the Sanhedrin challenged him for breaking the Sabbath laws. During the course of his explanation, Jesus compared himself to God. Just before the Jews were about to stone him, the Lord reminded them, "Is it not written in your law, I [God] said, Ye are gods?" (John 10:34). They could not deny that. King David, under the influence of the Holy Ghost, wrote, "I have said, Ye are gods; and all of you are children of the most High" (Psalms 82:6). Can it be stated any plainer? This may seem terribly simplistic, but do give it some thought. Puppies have the potential to grow up to be dogs. Kittens have the potential to grow up to be cats. So as sons and daughters of God, what do we have the potential to grow up to be? (See also Isaiah 41:23; Acts 17:29; Romans 8:16.)

The Apostle John clearly taught "now are we the sons of God" and when he, Jesus, returns, "we shall be like him." Therefore, it stands to reason that if Jesus is a God and if the righteous obedient will be like him, then they too will be gods. (See 1 John 3:2.)

In this same regard, we find a very compelling revelation as to the patriarchal order of godhood in the Book of Revelation. Here, John, while banished to the Isle of Patmos, received what we know as "The Revelation." In the opening, he addresses the seven churches in Asia with a bold testimony of Jesus Christ: "Who is the faithful witness, and the first begotten of the dead, and the prince of the kings of the earth. Unto him that loved us, and washed us from our sins in his own blood, And *hath made us kings and priests unto God and his Father*, to him be glory and dominion for ever and ever" (Revelation 1:5–6; italics added).

Reread that part in italics. He, Jesus Christ, has made us, his faithful followers, kings and priests to God and *His* (God's) Father! It does not read, He made us kings and priests to God, his (Jesus's) Father. There is an enormous difference between the two. The meaning is crystal clear! Have you, at any time, ever seen a father without a son or a son without a father?

At no time has the Church ever taught that we would grow up and replace God. It's as though these opponents think we are planning a coup to overthrow God our Eternal Father and remove Him from His throne.

Too many Mormon opponents quote the Ten Commandments in which God said, "I am the Lord thy God...Thou shalt have no other gods before me" (Exodus 20:2–3). At no time has the Church ever taught that we would grow up and replace God. It's as though these opponents think we are planning a coup to overthrow God our Eternal Father and remove Him from His throne. That simply isn't true. Look at it this way, using myself as an example. When I was born, I had a father. I was his son. He (and Mom) reared me and taught me and prepared me to become a father in my own time. Once I grew to adulthood, I moved away, got married and formed, with my wife, a home of my own, separate from that of my father's. When my wife Churé (pronounced Shu-ray) had our first child, it was a boy. I had a son; he had a father. A new, separate family from the one I had been born into had been formed. My becoming a father had no diminishing affect whatsoever on my father's family or the relationship between my father and me. It didn't lessen his role as my father. He was still my father. I could neither replace him nor move "before" him in any way, shape, or form. He was and always will be ahead of me. It's no different with us and God our Father. This is another way families are eternal. God the Father was and is and always will be our God and our Eternal Father. He will always and forever be before us in that capacity and in that same capacity we will, as gods, continue to worship Him. That will never change.

Taking into consideration this infinite and eternal point of view, how could anyone but the Father of our spirits be the author of the plan of salvation? It is also known as the Gospel of Jesus Christ. Paul refers to it as "the gospel of God …Concerning his Son Jesus Christ our Lord" (Romans 1:1, 3). Although Jesus implemented the plan, it is the Father's. Through the atonement, he, Jesus, became the author of salvation.

The second member of the Godhead is *God the Son*. Each one of us, including Jesus Christ, was born as a son or daughter of God. He is the Only Begotten in the flesh. His Father was God. His mother was Mary. He is the Son of God in the literal complete sense of the word. Of all the spirit children, he was the firstborn. Recording the words of the Father, the psalmists wrote, "Also I will make him my firstborn, higher than the kings of the earth" (Psalms 89:27). The Apostle Paul referred to him as "the firstborn among many brethren" (Romans 8:29) and again as "the firstborn of every creature" (Colossians 1:15).

God the Son is *God the Redeemer*. Salvation comes only through Jesus Christ and his atoning sacrifice. He ransomed mankind from the Fall of Adam. He is the *Savior* of the world: "And if any man hear my words, and believe not, I judge him not: for I came not to judge the world, but to save the world" (John 12:47).

When revealing himself to John the Revelator, Jesus referred to himself as "Alpha and Omega, the beginning and the ending" and a few versus later as "Alpha and Omega, the first and the last" (Revelation 1:8, 11; see also 1:17; 2:8; 21:6; 22:13). Alpha is the first letter in the Greek alphabet. Omega is the last letter of the Greek alphabet. Just as he said, "I am the first and the last." He is the first and only Savior, there will be no others. He is the last. All things are centered in Jesus Christ. All powers for life and salvation are centered in him. He, under the direction of his Father, initiated the plan of salvation and was its presiding authority at the beginning. Accordingly, he will be the presiding authority in the end at the final judgment. He is the finisher.

Jesus is our *Mediator*: "For there is one God, and one mediator between God and men, the man Christ Jesus" (1 Timothy 2:5). And he is our *Advocate* with the Father: "My little children, these things write I unto you, that ye sin not. And if any man sin, we have an advocate with the Father, Jesus Christ the righteous" (1 John 2:1).

Christ brings immortality to all men, redeeming them from temporal death through the resurrection. Through the atonement, he redeems the souls from spiritual death of all who believe in him and are baptized: "He that believeth and is baptized shall be saved; but he that believeth not shall be damned" (Mark 16:16; see Acts 2:38). In addition to this, he also requires us to obey his laws and commandments: "If ye love me, keep my commandments" (John 14:15; see also John 14:21, 23, and 24). In and by all these things he is the Savior of our bodies and the Redeemer of our souls.

Recently, a prominent minister in Dallas, Texas, delivered a sermon on Mormons saying, "It is a big deal if anybody names another way to be saved except through Jesus Christ." His statement is true, there is no other way. Also, his statement is false in that he was accusing The Church of Jesus Christ of Latter-day Saints of teaching "another way" for salvation. This simply goes to show how horribly uninformed this individual really is. Such statements reek of religious bigotry.

God the Son is also the *Creator*. As we saw earlier, under the direction of his Father, he did create this earth. Paul taught, "For by him were all things created, that are in heaven, and that are in earth, visible and invisible, whether they be thrones, or dominions, or principalities, or powers: all things were created by him, and for him: and he is before all things, and by him all things consist" (Colossians 1:16–17).

God the Son is the *Eternal Judge*. Speaking to some Jews who "sought the more to kill him" because of his declaration of divinity (John 5:18), the Lord said, "For the Father judgeth no man, but hath committed all judgment unto the Son: That all men should honour the Son, even as they honour the Father" (John 5:22–23).

God the Son is the *Father*. As we have seen above, he is the Father of the heaven and earth in that he was the *Creator* of them (just like Thomas Edison is the father of the electric light-bulb). He is the Father in that all who believe him are baptized and take upon them his name are adopted, as it were, into his family; they become his sons and daughters—they are spiritually begotten of him (born again through baptism). Finally, Jesus is the Father by divine investiture of authority. God *the* Father placed his own name, power, and authority on the Son (similar to power of attorney). Christ is empowered to act and speak in the first person as though he were the Father. Therefore, his words and acts become and are those of the Father. They are one in all things!

The third member of the Godhead is God *the Holy Ghost*. He is a Personage of Spirit. He doesn't have a tangible body as do the Father and the Son. Aside from this, he has the same personality, attributes, and perfections as do the other two members of the Godhead. Because of the nature of his duties and responsibilities within the Godhead, it's necessary that he not, at this time, have a tangible body, else how could he, figuratively speaking, dwell in the hearts of those who have accepted Christ as their Savior? He, a Spirit being, speaks to our

Joseph Smith couldn't have made up that story about seeing "two Personages," not based on the information he had available to him. He didn't get his information from the Bible as it was being taught at that time, either.

spirits in only a way a spirit could—Spirit speaking to spirit.

The Holy Ghost is the *Comforter*. Jesus promised his followers that those who keep his commandments would receive "the Comforter, which is the Holy Ghost, whom the Father will send in my name" (John 14:26).

The Holy Ghost is a *Testator* and *Revelator*. He is God's minister. It's his job to teach, testify, and bear witness to the Father and the Son (see John 15:26) and the reality and divinity of the Gospel of Jesus Christ. He also reveals all things—all truth—to those who earnestly seek after it. "The Comforter, which is the Holy Ghost, whom the Father will send in my name, he *shall teach you all things, and bring all things to your remembrance*, whatsoever I have said unto you" (John 14:26; italics added). The Holy Ghost reveals the mind and will of God to worthy men and women (Acts 1:2). It is through the Holy Ghost that God speaks to his sons and daughters. Some examples are found in Luke 1:41, 67; 2:25–26; 12:12; Acts 2:4; 4:8; 4:31, to name a few.

As to the physical nature of God the Father and His Son, I had mentioned in the previous chapter, Joseph Smith couldn't have made up that story about seeing "two Personages," not based on the information he had available to him. He didn't get his information from the Bible as it was being taught at that time, either. However, Mormons believe that the Bible proves Joseph's account and his story is, in fact, harmonized by the Bible. How?

Let's start "in the beginning." In the first chapter of the first book of the Bible, we read, "And God said, Let *us* make man in *our* image, after *our* likeness. So God created man in his own image, in the image of God created he him; male and female created he them" (Genesis 1:26–27; italics added).

This brings up two questions. The first: Who is God addressing in this verse? (We'll answer that shortly.) The second: What do the words *image* and *likeness* mean? The Merriam-Webster Online Dictionary defines image as "a reproduction or imitation of the form of a person or thing; *especially*: an imitation in solid form." The same dictionary defines likeness as "the quality or state of being like."

Many have tried to explain away these verses in Genesis by saying this was a reference to a spiritual image and likeness. Yet those individuals who teach this also say God is without "parts." If God is some singular, nebulous, gaseous cloud without form, we too would be without parts and without form, being nebulous, gaseous clouds, because we were created in His image and likeness—being "an imitation in solid form." How, then, could we be made in His image and likeness if this weren't true? The same prophet (Moses) who wrote the above passages also wrote, "And Adam lived an hundred and thirty years, and begat a son in his own *likeness*, after his *image*; and called his name Seth" (Genesis 5:3; italics added). So the words image and likeness as used in the first passages either have the same meaning or they have a different meaning from those same words used in the second passage. It can't be both. And certainly Moses not only understood the meaning of these two words, he also understood how to use them.

Referring again to the writings of Moses, what was it that he, Aaron, Nadab, Abihu, and seventy of the elders of Israel saw when they went up on the mount? "And they saw the God of Israel: and there was under his *feet* as it were a paved work of a sapphire stone, and as it were the body of heaven in his clearness" (Exodus 24:10; italics added). And elsewhere, Moses recorded, "And the Lord spake unto Moses *face to face*, as a man speaketh unto his friend" (Exodus 33:11, italics added; see also Matthew 18:10). Just like Moses, Joseph Smith spoke with God and His Son "face to face, as a man speaketh unto his friend."

In his Epistle to the Hebrews, Paul made it abundantly clear the kind of personage God is. He taught that Jesus, the Eternal Father's Son, was in "the brightness of his glory, and the *express image of his person*" and that when he had ascended into heaven, after his forty-day postresurrection ministry, "sat down on the right hand of the Majesty on high" (Hebrews 1:3; italics added). First of all, the word *express* used here as an adjective means "explicit," "exact," and "precise." So that means God the Father looks like Jesus Christ, which means He has a tangible body. Secondly, it stands to reason that the only way the resurrected Lord could sit down on the Father's right-hand side was if the Father had a corporal body with a right-hand side on which he, Jesus, could sit.

Next, I submit to you the testimony of Stephen as it was recorded by Paul. Remember, Stephen had been declaring to the Jews their wickedness before the Sanhedrin and just prior to being stoned to death he, being full of the Holy Ghost, "looked up stedfastly into heaven, and saw the glory of God, and Jesus standing on the right hand of God, And said, Behold, I see the heavens opened, and the Son of man standing on the right hand of God" (Acts 7:55–56; italics added). Stephen not only saw that God has a body of parts, but he also saw two distinct and separate personages: one being God the Son standing on the right-hand side of the other, the other being God the Father. How can we deny his testimony, he being "a man full of faith and of the Holy Ghost" (Acts 6:5) while insisting that God the Father is without a tangible body of parts?

This third example is one of the most unique and definitive testimonies of the separateness of the three members of the Godhead. It takes place immediately following the baptism of Jesus by John the Baptist: "And [1] Jesus, when he was baptized, went up straightway out of the water: and, lo, the heavens were opened unto him, and he saw [2] the Spirit of God descending like a dove, and lighting upon him:

"And lo [3] a voice from heaven, saying, This is my beloved Son, in whom I am well pleased" (Matthew 3:16–17).

It's plain to see here each distinct member of the Godhead as recorded. The first is the second member, that being Jesus, is coming up out of the water. The second is the third member, that being the Holy Ghost, descending like a dove. The third is the first member, being the Eternal Father, who speaks from heaven pronouncing His love and approval for His "beloved Son." This being the case, how can anyone maintain that these three separate individuals are one in body, whatever form it may be?

Next, let's turn to the Lord's great intercessory prayer found in John 17. It begins with, "These words spake Jesus, and lifted up his eyes to heaven, and said, *Father*, the hour is come; glorify *thy* Son, that *thy* Son also may glorify *thee*." (John 17:1; italics added).

Question: If the Father and the Son are the same person, to whom is Jesus praying?

Answer: He is praying to Him who is his God and his Father. He is praying to Him that is our God and our Father (see John 20:17). He isn't praying to himself!

The Lord continues, "And this is life eternal, that they might know *thee* the only true God, *and Jesus Christ*, whom *thou* hast sent" (John 17:3; italics added). Consider this, I have a son. His name is Dustin. Picture, if you will, Dustin has arrived at college. He has made new friends. He calls me on the phone and says, "I hope my new friends will get to know you, Dad, and me, whom you have sent to college." Again, the reference to two individuals is clear. But just in case. The Lord continues, "*I* have glorified *thee* on the earth: *I* have finished the work which *thou* gavest me to do" (John 17:4; italics added). He, Jesus, one distinct individual, has finished the work which the Father, another distinct individual, charged him to accomplish. If Jesus and the Father were the same person, why would Jesus return and report as we do to someone that has give us an assignment? It stands to reason, if the two were one person, such reporting would be unnecessary. Do you report back to yourself once you have completed a task you had initiated?

Then the Lord made a statement that helps substantiate all we've been discussing here. When he said, "And now, O Father, glorify thou *me* with *thine own self* with the glory which *I* had with *thee* before the world was" (John 17:5; italics added), again, he acknowledged this Being to whom he is praying as *his* Father, showing that he and his Father are two individual beings. He obviously differentiates between himself, "me," and the Father, "thine own self." Not only that, but we also learn, by listening to the Savior of all mankind as he makes all this as clear as it can be, that they are two distinct and separate beings because he, Jesus, was with God, the Father, before the world was created! This brings up my earlier question. When God said, "Let *us* make man in our image, after *our* likeness," who was he speaking to? Here we have the answer. He was speaking to the premortal Jesus—Jehovah.

In case there are any remaining doubts, here is another quote from the Lord himself that clearly shows the separateness of the Father and the Son: "I can of *mine own self* do nothing …because *I* seek not *mine own will*, but *the will of the Father* which hath sent *me*" (John 5:30; italics added). Here, three facts are evident: (1) Christ has again plainly separated himself from his Father; (2) the Lord has also separated his will from the will of his Father—two individual wills, the lesser submitting to the greater; (3) Jesus says that he was "sent" from the Father. In order for a person to be sent from the presence of another, there has to be at least two beings present to begin with, isn't that correct?

With these witnesses from the Lord Jesus Christ himself, we can, with total confidence, see that Joseph Smith's testimony of being visited by "two Personages" proclaiming to be God the Father and God the Son, and that they are two distinct and separate Beings, is a doctrinal fact. The Bible proves it!

Now, as sure as I'm sitting here writing this, there is someone sitting out there reading this thinking, "Yeah, but what about John 1:18 that says, 'No man hath seen God at any time; the only begotten Son, which is in the bosom of the Father, he hath declared him'? And what about Paul's mentioning 'the invisible God' in Colossians 1:15?"

Okay, let's start with the last passage first. If we study Paul's teaching further rather than taking it out of context, we learn that he, Paul, had the same understanding that John had, that being God is indeed invisible to men in general, especially to those who don't believe (exhibiting a lack of faith) God can manifest Himself to them. However, Paul fully understood that God has and does show Himself to the prophet (and anyone else He deems worthy). Paul made it clear that Moses had seen the "invisible God" when he said,

"By faith he [Moses] forsook Egypt, not fearing the wrath of the king: for he endured, as *seeing* him [God] who is invisible" (Hebrews 11:27; italics added).

Speaking of Paul's knowledge, let's revisit Hebrews 1:1–3 which reads,

> God, who at sundry times and in divers manners spake in time past unto the fathers by the prophets,
>
> Hath in these last days spoken unto us by his Son, whom he hath appointed heir of all things, by whom also he made the worlds;
>
> "Who being the brightness of his glory, and the express image of his person, and upholding all things by the word of his power, when he had by himself purged our sins, sat down on the right hand of the Majesty on high.

Again, we see the separate nature of God the Father and God the Son. But I want you to focus on something in verse 3, that being Paul's declaration that Jesus's being is in "the express image of his [God the Father's] person." That is to say, "Jesus looks just like his Father." So let me ask you: How did Paul know that? By what means did he gain this unique piece of information? What experience would Paul have had to have in order to *know* that Jesus is the "express image" of God the Father? Think about it.

Now, regarding the first question, I have already shown that Moses saw God. Remember, we've already learned that God is not the author of confusion or a God of contradictions (see 1 Corinthians 14:33).

Getting back to John 1:18, Joseph Smith, a prophet of God, operating under divine direction with full authority and exercising the gift of revelation as all past prophets have while under the influence of the Holy Ghost, translated that verse to read: "And no man hath seen God at any time, except he hath borne record of the Son; for except it is through him no man can be saved" (JST John 1:19). Joseph explained elsewhere that "no man has seen God at any time in the flesh, except quickened by the Spirit of God" (Doctrine and Covenants 67:11). This doctrine is further explained by Moses as revealed to the Prophet Joseph when he translated the Book of Moses: "But now mine own eyes have beheld God; but not my natural, but my spiritual eyes, for my natural eyes could not have beheld; for I should have withered and died in his presence; but his glory was upon me; and I beheld his face, for I was transfigured before him" (Moses 1:11).

This makes perfect sense, doesn't it? Well, consider how this very doctrine is supported by verses in the Bible.

> And after six days Jesus taketh Peter, James, and John his brother, and bringeth them up into an high mountain apart,
>
> And was transfigured before them: and his face did shine as the sun, and his raiment was white as the light.
>
> And, behold, there appeared unto them Moses and Elias talking with him.
>
> Then answered Peter, and said unto Jesus, Lord, it is good for us to be here: if thou wilt, let us make here three tabernacles; one for thee, and one for Moses, and one for Elias.
>
> While he yet spake, behold, a bright cloud overshadowed them: and behold a voice out of the cloud, which said, This is my beloved Son, in whom I am well pleased; hear ye him.

And when the disciples heard it, they fell on their face, and were sore afraid.

And Jesus came and touched them, and said, Arise, and be not afraid.

And when they had lifted up their eyes, they saw no man, save Jesus only.

And as they came down from the mountain, Jesus charged them, saying, Tell the vision to no man, until the Son of man be risen again from the dead. (Matthew 17:1–9)

In these verses Jesus has taken Peter, James, and John up on a "high mountain" where they stand in the presence of Jesus, Moses, Elias, and most importantly, God the Father! They were "overshadowed" by a cloud. From that cloud God spoke to them. But wait a minute. How can that be? God speaking to Moses said, "Thou canst not see my face: for there shall no man see me, and live" (Exodus 33:20). How can that be? Moses had seen God and spoke with him "face to face," and he didn't die. There is only one answer. Those faithful few who have had the privilege of seeing God have undergone a transfiguration—an overshadowing, a quickening by the Spirit—that enabled them to withstand His presence without dying. Think about it, what purpose would be served by God revealing Himself to His servants if they died in the process? How can dead men bear testimony to the reality of God's character and His nature if they are consumed in His presence? That would throw a definite wrench in works, wouldn't it?

Another idea that many Christians find confusing is John's reference to God as a spirit: "God is a Spirit: and they that worship him must worship him in spirit and in truth" (John 4:24). Again, with a proper understanding of spiritual matters, this shouldn't be all that confusing. Paul taught, "We are also his offspring. Forasmuch then as we are the offspring of God" (Acts 17:28–29). Each one of us is a literal spirit son or daughter of God. We are spirits clothed with bodies of flesh and blood and bones. If John says we are to "worship [God] in spirit and truth," does that imply that we should cast off our bodies in order for us to worship him "in spirit"? Of course not! We couldn't do it if we wanted to. The noun spirit used in this context refers to an "essential principle." Hence, we are to worship God in the "essential principle" of spiritual things, or eternal principles, meaning those as established by God the Father, the author of the plan of salvation.

Another passage from Paul found in 1 Corinthians may help to explain what I'm saying: "But he that is joined unto the Lord is one spirit" (1 Corinthians 6:17).

This "oneness" or "being one" has been the source of much confusion and misunderstanding as well. It seems that the Bible has several of references to the idea there is only one God. Here are some examples.

> And the scribe said unto him, Well, Master, thou hast said the truth: for there is one God; and there is none other but he. (Mark 12:32)

> One God and Father of all, who is above all, and through all, and in you all. (Ephesians 4:6)

> Thou believest that there is one God; thou doest well: the devils also believe, and tremble. (James 2:19)

These verses, when taken out of context, appear to be stating unequivocally that there is only one God and none other. But haven't we learned that the scriptures are like a jigsaw puzzle?

When we open a jigsaw puzzle box, we see hundreds, if not thousands, of individual pieces, none of which can stand on its own revealing what the full picture actually is. We might even find several pieces that fit together perfectly, giving us an indication of a tree, a flower, an eye, or a boat. Still, those few pieces don't illustrate a full or accurate image of what the whole picture really is. It's not any different with the scriptures.

We have already seen in the previous pages that there are two Personages with tangible bodies in the Godhead, and one who is a Spirit Personage. In spite of those scriptures above, there is yet another scripture that supports the fact of two separate beings: "But to us there is but *one God, the Father*, of whom are all things, and we in him; *and one Lord Jesus Christ*, by whom are all things, and we by him" (1 Corinthians 8:6; italics added). Once again, two separate beings have been revealed. Can it be any more simple?

We could go on at length with this, but in order to save time and space, let's refer to a definitive source, Jesus Christ himself, and see what he has to say in this regard. We'll return to his great intercessory prayer. As Jesus prayed to his Father, he thanked Him for the apostles that had been given to him, and he asked that God would keep them "that they may be one, as *we* are" (John 17:11; italics added). The pronoun *we* is plural—"you and I." He continues to pray for them, saying, "Neither pray I for these alone, but for them also which shall believe on me through their word;

"That they all may be one; as thou, Father, art in me, and I in thee, that they also may be one in us: that the world may believe that thou hast sent me" (John 17:20–21).

It's obvious the Lord isn't speaking of them being one person. Christ wasn't praying that his apostles would lose their individuality and become melded into one being even if such a change were possible, which it wasn't and isn't. What the Lord desired was that they should all be united in heart, mind, spirit, and purpose, just like he, his Father, and the Holy Ghost are united in heart, mind, spirit, and purpose.

They have the same mind, they have the same understanding, they have the same thoughts, they speak the same words, and they execute the same deeds. What one would think, the other two would think. What one would say, the other two would say exactly the same thing. What one would do, the other two would do under the same circumstances.

The three individual members of the Godhead possess the same character, attributes, and perfections. They are unified in all things—not some things or most things, but in *all* things. That is how they are one.

Yes, Jesus, during his mortal ministry, was the manifestation of the Father, and that means God the Father was revealing Himself to men through His Son. While in the upper room, prior to the Last Supper, Jesus declared, "If ye had known me, ye should have known my Father also: and from henceforth ye know him, and have seen him" (John 14:7). Then the Apostle Philip, still confused by the statement, said, "Lord, shew us the Father, and it sufficeth us" (John 14:8). The Lord's reply seemed to indicate that he may have been a little miffed with Philip's lack of understanding. He asked, "Have I been so long time with you, and yet hast thou not known me, Philip?" Then Jesus goes on to explain, "He that hath seen me hath seen the Father" (John 14:9). To know one is to know the other. To see one is to see the other. If you believe Jesus is the Christ, then you believe that God is the Eternal Father. "And he that receiveth me receiveth him that sent me" (Matthew 10:40; John 13:20).

To those that believe in the Son, who also believe in the

Father, the Father sends the Holy Ghost to sanctify them that they may be fit to dwell in their presence forever.

So where is the problem? Why the apparent inconsistency as it pertains to the nature of God? There can only be one answer—*man*.

Turning to the writings of Paul once more, "Eye hath not seen, nor ear heard, neither have entered into the heart of man, the things which God hath prepared for them that love him" (1 Corinthians 2:9). Simply put, the common, fallen, and mortal man cannot even begin to comprehend the things God has in store for him. "But God hath revealed them unto us *by* his Spirit: for the Spirit searcheth all things, yea, the deep things of God" (1 Corinthians 2:10; italics added). God has, does, and will reveal Himself and His mysteries to those who believe and exercise faith in His Son (see Mark 9:23; Luke 1:37), and this is done by and through the third member of the Godhead, the Spirit or Holy Ghost. "For what man knoweth the things of a man, save [by] the spirit of man which is in him? even so the things of God knoweth no man, but [by] the Spirit of God" (1 Corinthians 2:11). Here we learn another eternal truth: the Holy Ghost, Spirit, is the testator, witness, teacher of all truth (see John 14:26).

"Which things also we speak, not in the words which man's wisdom teacheth, but which the Holy Ghost teacheth; comparing spiritual things with spiritual.

"But the natural man receiveth not the things of the Spirit of God: for they are foolishness unto him: neither can he know them, because they are spiritually discerned" (1 Corinthians 2:13–14).

Here Paul is saying, We teach God's truths, not using man's words or man's wisdom. He also referred to this as "fleshy wisdom." (See 2 Corinthians 1:12.) He goes on as if to say, We teach eternal truths by the words and the wisdom of God given to us by the power and gift of the Holy Ghost. Men who rely upon their own knowledge, wisdom, or understanding cannot understand the things of God because they sound too ridiculous. Those men who rely solely upon their own puny intelligence and finite understanding will never comprehend the infinite things of God because they are only understood by the Holy Ghost revealing them to us—Spirit speaking to our spirits.

As we have seen, scripture comes from God through revelation to His chosen servants. In order to fully and completely comprehend scripture, that too requires revelation. There are too many different interpretations of the same verses today between the various churches. Why is that? Could it be because they have, through their own disbeliefs and lack of faith, sealed the heavens?

Now, as to whether or not God the Father is a perfected man who was once mortal, give the following some additional thought. The restored Gospel of Jesus Christ teaches that God is a perfected man, that God once lived as a mortal man on an earth not unlike this one. For some reason, this offends a great many other Christians. Jesus is a God, is he not? He lived as a mortal upon this earth, did he not? He suffered mortality just as the rest of us do. He was born as we were: "And she brought forth her firstborn son, and wrapped him in swaddling clothes, and laid him in a manger" (Luke 2:7). He grew up as we have: "And the child grew, and waxed strong in spirit, filled with wisdom: and the grace of God was upon him" (Luke 2:40). He was fatigued as we are: "And he was in the hinder part of the ship, asleep on a pillow" (Mark 4:38). He felt sorrow as we do: "Jesus wept" (John 11:35). He loved as we do: "Now Jesus loved Martha, and her sister, and Lazarus" (John 11:5).

During his mortality, he experienced everything we experience (and then some), except he never gave in to Satan's temptations as we do. He even died as all do: "And when Jesus had cried with a loud voice, he said, Father, into thy hands I commend my spirit: and having said thus, he gave up the ghost" (Luke 23:46). And was resurrected as all of us will be: "Jesus Christ of Nazareth, whom ye crucified, whom God raised from the dead" (Acts 4:10); "For as in Adam all die, even so in Christ shall all be made alive" (1 Corinthians 15:22).

It is clearly evident that God the Son was a mortal man, who was born, lived, died, and was resurrected. And after he was resurrected, he, with his tangible body, appeared to his apostles in the upper room and told them, "Handle me . . . for a spirit hath not flesh and bones, as ye see me have" (Luke 24:39). They handled his resurrected body. He asked for some broiled fish and honeycomb and did eat. Later, Thomas, the doubter, thrust his hand into the Lord's side and felt the imprints of the nails in his hands and feet. Forty days later, after his postresurrection ministry, the apostles stood and watched as Jesus, with his tangible body of flesh and bones, ascended to heaven (see Acts 1:9).

How is it possible that anyone can teach that God the Son was never a mortal man living on earth? How is it possible that anyone can teach that God the Son does not have a body of flesh and bones? We have just clearly seen that such teachings are unmistakably incorrect.

This being the case (and given that we have seen that God the Father and God the Son are two distinct, individual personages, who are the same in *all* character, attributes, perfections, who are in the "express image" of each other, and since God the Father is above God the Son), it only stands to reason that God the Father too has a body of flesh and bones, doesn't it?

Of course it does! Jesus himself declared, "Verily, verily, I say unto you, The Son can do nothing of himself, *but what he seeth the Father do: for what things soever he doeth, these also doeth the Son likewise*" (John 5:19; italics added). He, Jesus, has done only that which he has seen his Father (God) do. Therefore, if Jesus did what God the Father had done, then God the Father at some previous time had gone through mortality just as Jesus had. How could it be otherwise?

And that is the testimony that Joseph Smith bore from the very beginning of his work. His knowledge of this truth came to him through the God-given experience he had that spring morning in a grove of trees in upstate New York in 1820.

With a prophet in place, the first truth to be restored was the correct character and nature of God the Eternal Father, God His Son Jesus Christ, and God the Holy Ghost.

Restitution of All Things

*A*s we've already seen, the prophets foresaw a universal falling away from the truth. This was the condition of the world at the time Joseph Smith sought an answer to his question regarding which church to join.

Revisiting Isaiah's prophesy,

> Wherefore the Lord said, Forasmuch as this people draw near me with their mouth, and with their lips do honour me, but have removed their heart far from me, and their fear toward me is taught by the precept of men:
>
> Therefore, behold, I will proceed to do a marvellous work among this people, even *a marvellous work and a wonder:* for the wisdom of their wise men shall perish, and the understanding of their prudent men shall be hid. (Isaiah 29:13–14; italics added)

What, in your mind, would constitute a marvelous work and a wonder?

You'd think that those who claim to be Christians, followers of Jesus Christ, those who believe the Bible to be the Word of God, would be excited to learn that such an event had taken place as promised. "What? Are you crazy? How can such a thing be?" you ask. "What's wrong with Mormons?"

The marvelous work of the restitution of all things was the

restoration of the complete, full Gospel of Christ. Consider the words of John the Revelator. At one point during the course of the revelation he was called by the angel to "come up hither" and the angel proceeded to show him "things which must be hereafter," things which must come to pass *prior* to the Second Coming (Revelation 4:1). Later in that same vision, he declared, "I saw another angel fly in the midst of heaven, having the everlasting gospel to preach unto them that dwell on the earth, and to every nation, and kindred, and tongue, and people" (Revelation 14:6). Had the Gospel in its fullness existed anywhere on the earth, there would not be any reason for an angel to restore it, would there?

Along these same lines, let's look to the Old Testament prophet Malachi, who also saw the promised day of restoration. To him God said, "Behold, I will send my messenger, and he shall prepare the way before me: and the Lord, whom ye seek, shall suddenly come to his temple, even the messenger of the covenant, whom ye delight in: behold, he shall come, saith the Lord of hosts" (Malachi 3:1). This obviously has reference to the Second Coming and not Jesus's birth as he has to "suddenly come to his temple," which he didn't do at his birth. Also, prior to the restoration, there were no temples on the earth for him to come suddenly to!

Part of the restitution included the restoration of the office of prophet to the earth. The Old Testament prophet Amos affirmed, "Surely the Lord God will do nothing, but he revealeth his secret unto his servants the prophets" (Amos 3:7). That's a pretty straightforward statement. It makes perfect sense too, doesn't it? What kind of God would He be if, for example, He had flooded the earth without warning the prophet Noah? What kind of God would He be if He hadn't warned Lot of the impending fate of Sodom and Gomorrah before raining down fire and brimstone? What kind of God would He be if He hadn't warned the people of the coming of the Messiah through the prophet John the Baptist? So Heavenly Father is true to His word. Such is the case in the Dispensation of the Fullness of Times.

Before God could begin this "marvellous work," he would have to reveal His plan to the prophet. But there was no prophet on the earth at the time. That means before He could begin, He would have to call one to stand as a prophet to the people as He had done in times past.

It doesn't make any sense that God would call a man who was so deeply entrenched in the doctrines and traditions of men that he couldn't (wouldn't) be taught (what at the time would be) new doctrine. As Jesus stated, "Neither do men put new wine into old bottles: else the bottles break, and the wine runneth out, and the bottles perish: but they put new wine into new bottles, and both are preserved" (Matthew 9:17). On the other hand, by choosing a young man who was doctrinally untainted, humble, and malleable, the Lord could then teach him whatsoever was necessary. It would, indeed, be putting new wine into a new bottle. God's ways are not our ways: "'For my thoughts are not your thoughts, neither are your ways my ways,' saith the Lord."

"'For as the heavens are higher than the earth, so are my ways higher than your ways, and my thoughts than your thoughts'" (Isaiah 55:8–9).

You might ask, "Why would God call an inexperienced youth like Joseph Smith to be His new prophet?" The answer is God knew us all before we were born. He knew our nature and disposition while we lived with Him as His spirit children. Remember, He chose Jesus "before the world was" (John 17:5) to be the Savior of the world.

It was for this same reason that God selected Jeremiah to be a prophet: "Before I formed thee in the belly I knew thee; and before thou camest forth out of the womb I sanctified thee, and I ordained thee a prophet unto the nations" (Jeremiah 1:5).

If God's announcement to Jeremiah is true, and there's no reason to think otherwise, then how could Jeremiah be known, called, and ordained *before* he was born if he didn't exist?

This is why the restored Gospel couldn't rely upon the Bible alone for its reorganization. This is why the restored Gospel would require one who wasn't relying upon biblical teachings alone at the time to be an instrument in God's hand to carry out such a marvelous work.

It had been three years since Joseph had his vision of the Father and the Son. Just by telling those around him of his experience in the grove, seeing the Father and the Son and having them speak to him, he had brought "great sorrow" (JSH 1:23) upon himself in the form of persecution from those who professed to be religious as well as those who weren't. In spite of his divine experience, we learn from him that he was as much a boy as any were.

> During the space of time which intervened between the time I had the vision and the year eighteen hundred and twenty-three…I frequently fell into many foolish errors, and displayed the weakness of youth, and the foibles of human nature; which, I am sorry to say, led me into divers temptations, offensive in the sight of God. In making this confession, no one need suppose me guilty of any great or malignant sins. A disposition to commit such was never in my nature.
>
> In consequence of these things, I often felt

condemned for my weakness and imperfections; when, on the evening of the above-mentioned twenty-first of September, after I had retired to my bed for the night, I betook myself to prayer and supplication to Almighty God for forgiveness of all my sins and follies, and also for a manifestation to me, that I might know of my state and standing before him.

While I was thus in the act of calling upon God, I discovered a light appearing in my room, which continued to increase until the room was lighter than at noonday, when immediately a personage appeared at my bedside, standing in the air, for his feet did not touch the floor.

He called me by name, and said unto me that he was a messenger sent from the presence of God to me, and that his name was Moroni; that God had a work for me to do; and *that my name should be had for good and evil among all nations, kindreds, and tongues, or that it should be both good and evil spoken of among all people.* (JSH 1:28–33; italics added)

Let's take a closer look at what the angel Moroni (the angel that John the Revelator and Malachi saw in vision) had prophesied. Joseph was told that all nations, kindreds, tongues, and people (that pretty well covers everybody) would know his name and they would speak of him either with kindness and respect, or they would speak lies and evil about him. Has that prophesy come to pass? It certainly has! None of the Protestant reformers can make such a claim as that.

Why should anyone be angry because God spoke to Joseph Smith? If they don't believe it happened, then why all the

The devil, Lucifer, was a spirit son of God. Like us, he had his agency—the freedom to choose good over evil—in the premortal existence. He chose evil.

resentment? If they're right, they have nothing to fear. So what is it they fear? Why are prophets persecuted? "Which of the prophets have not your fathers persecuted?" was the question Stephen asked of those who stoned him. He provided the answer for them, "They have slain them which shewed before of the coming of the Just One; of whom ye have been now the betrayers and murderers" (Acts 7:52). The prophets are persecuted (even killed) because they testify of the reality of Jesus Christ, and for that reason alone.

Before we can attempt to answer why anyone would do such a thing, we must take into consideration something we haven't yet discussed. That's the role of Lucifer—who he is and what he does.

We briefly touched upon this in chapter 3. As there is opposition in all things, so Jesus Christ has his opposite in the devil, which literally means "slanderer." The devil, Lucifer, was a spirit son of God. Like us, he had his agency—the freedom to choose good over evil—in the premortal existence. He chose evil. He chose to oppose Heavenly Father's Plan and, by doing so, rebelled against God. There was a war in heaven, and a "third part of the stars [spirit children] of heaven" followed the devil and they were cast out of heaven and down to the newly formed earth. This war was a war of words and ideologies. It was a rebellion against God and His plan. Lucifer declared that he would redeem all men, but in doing so he would deny them their agency, the ability to choose good over evil. That war between the good and evil continues here on earth. "Woe to the inhabiters of the earth," John the Revelator declared, "for the devil is come down unto you...to make war...[with those] which keep the commandments of God, and have the testimony of Jesus Christ" (see Revelation 12:4–17).

As a result of their rebellion and having been cast out, Lucifer and those who followed him had forever forfeited the opportunity to be born into mortality and receive tangible bodies. For them, there is no hope of ever returning to live with their Father in heaven. They are spiritually dead.

Here on earth, Lucifer and his angels put into the minds of men (spirit speaking to spirit) the ideas of false worship (Revelation 13:4). Any form of worship other than that as set up by Christ, as Paul declared, is false worship: "The things which the Gentiles sacrifice, they sacrifice to devils, and not to God: and I would not that ye should have fellowship with devils.

"Ye cannot drink the cup of the Lord, and the cup of the devils: ye cannot be partakers of the Lord's table, and of the table of devils" (1 Corinthians 10:20–21).

Since Satan and his angels have no hope whatsoever of returning to their Heavenly Father's presence, they are hell-bent (excuse the pun) on making sure that they prevent as many of us as they can from doing so as well. They know that salvation is in Christ (see Luke 8:28; James 2:19) and where there are prophets, there is salvation, and where there are no prophets, there is no salvation available. So is it any wonder that Satan hates prophets and desires to bring about their destruction?

Persecuting prophets is a form of false worship. Consider again the words of the Lord to his disciples: "The time cometh that whosoever killeth you will think that he doeth God service" (John 16:2). Imagine that! In this dispensation most of the persecution that is heaped upon the Mormons has been, is planned, and is led by leaders of other churches. There is no doubt in my mind that some of them are sincere in their belief (I have read too many of their writings) that by destroying Mormonism they will free people, like me, from what they regard to be its evil delusions. Such was the case in Jesus's day, such was the case in Joseph Smith's day, and such is the case today. And what did Jesus say of those who carried out this work?

> Woe unto you, scribes and Pharisees, hypocrites! because ye build the tombs of the prophets, and garnish the sepulchres of the righteous,
>
> And say, If we had been in the days of our fathers, we would not have been partakers with them in the blood of the prophets.
>
> Wherefore ye be witnesses unto yourselves, that ye are the children of them which killed the prophets.
>
> Fill ye up then the measure of your fathers.
>
> Ye serpents, ye generation of vipers, how can ye escape the damnation of hell? (Matthew 23:29–33)

That's a pretty scathing indictment. So much for those who persecute prophets. History, both ancient and recent, has borne out the truth and reality of the prophecy given to Joseph by the angel Moroni. After many false imprisonments and many trials, all based on false charges brought against him, Joseph Smith was never found guilty of any wrongdoing. In their frustration his enemies declared, "If the law will not reach them, powder and ball can" (*History of the Church*, Vol. 6, p. 549). On June 27, 1844, a wicked mob stormed the Carthage Jail in Illinois and shot Joseph Smith and his brother Hyrum to death, thinking that by killing them the Church would slip into oblivion. This was the same logic used by the Sanhedrin when they plotted to crucify the Christ and again when they discussed killing the apostles. They all, in both dispensations, should have heeded the words of the wise Gamaliel when he warned,

> Ye men of Israel, take heed to yourselves what ye intend to do as touching these men.
>
> And now I say unto you, Refrain from these men, and let them alone: for if this counsel or this work be of men, it will come to nought:
>
> But if it be of God, ye cannot overthrow it; lest haply ye be found even to fight against God (Acts 5:35, 38–39; see Acts 5:26–39).

Okay, let's get back to the restitution. When the angel Moroni had appeared to Joseph, he declared that "God had a work for [Joseph] to do." The angel went on to say,

> There was a book deposited, written upon gold plates, giving an account of the former inhabitants of this continent, and the source from whence they sprang. He also said that the fullness of the everlasting Gospel was contained in it, as delivered by the Savior to the ancient inhabitants; also, that there were two stones in silver bows—and these stones, fastened to a breastplate, constituted what is called the Urim and Thummim—deposited with the plates; and the possession and use of these stones were what constituted "seers" in ancient or former times; and that God had prepared them for the purpose of translating the book.
>
> While he was conversing with me about the plates, the vision was opened to my mind that I could see the place where the plates were deposited, and that so clearly and distinctly that I knew the place again when I visited it. (JSH 1:34–35, 42)

This work of translating the book written upon gold plates (which would be known as the Book of Mormon) was to be, in part, the means by which God would reveal His truths to the earth and its inhabitants through His newly called prophet. It was what we would refer to today as a tutorial. As he moved through the translation process, many doctrinal questions would arise that would require further explanation, which in turn would send Joseph back to God in prayer to seek an answer to these new questions.

The Book of Mormon is "Another Testament of Jesus Christ." The coming forth of the Book of Mormon fulfills ancient prophecy. Prophesying the first destruction of Jerusalem, the prophet Isaiah declared, "Woe to Ariel, to Ariel, the city where David dwelt…I will distress Ariel, and there shall be heaviness and sorrow.

"And thou shalt be brought down, and shalt speak out of the ground, and thy speech shall be low out of the dust, and thy voice shall be, as of one that hath a familiar spirit, out of the ground, and thy speech shall whisper out of the dust" (Isaiah 29:1–2, 4).

Isaiah foresaw the destruction of Ariel, or Jerusalem. He saw the inhabitants, he saw how they would be brought down and would speak out of the ground. Their speech would be "low out of the dust"; their voice would have a "familiar spirit," coming out of the ground; their speech would "whisper out of the dust." How could the dead speak "out of the ground" or "low out of the dust"? That would have to be by the written word, and that record would have to be buried in the ground as were the golden plates.

Long before there was a Bible and long before there was a Book of Mormon, David, the psalmist, wrote, "Truth shall spring out of the earth; and righteousness shall look down from heaven" (Psalms 85:11). How, in what manner, might truth "spring out of the earth," and "righteousness...look down from heaven"? The answer to both questions is given through the Book of Mormon.

Jesus, in speaking to his disciples, acknowledged, "I lay down my life for the sheep. And other sheep I have, which are not of this fold: *them also I must bring, and they shall hear my voice; and there shall be one fold, and one shepherd*" (John 10:15–16; italics added).

How often do we read something, especially in the scriptures, and not immediately see what is being said? There were other sheep—other followers—who hadn't yet heard his voice, but were required to be brought into the fold. Where might those "other sheep" be?

We know that God made certain covenants (two-way promises) with Abraham, Isaac, Jacob (Israel), and his twelve sons

1. Reuben
2. Simeon
3. Levi
4. Judah
5. Issachar
6. Zebulun
7. Joseph (Ephraim and Manasseh)
8. Benjamin
9. Dan
10. Naphtali
11. Gad
12. Asher

Each of these sons was the head of a tribe comprising the house of Israel. A proper study of these covenants clearly shows the outstanding promises given to Judah and Joseph.

There is considerable confusion today in this regard because of the misapplication of the name *Israel*. All too often it is misused as referring to the Jews or the house of Judah alone, forgetting that Judah was only one of twelve. Reuben, the eldest son, lost his birthright due to transgression. "Now the sons of Reuben the firstborn of Israel, (for he was the firstborn; but, forasmuch as he defiled his father's bed, his birthright was given unto the sons of Joseph the son of Israel: and the genealogy is not to be reckoned after the birthright. For Judah prevailed above his brethren, and of him came the chief ruler; but the birthright was Joseph's)" (1 Chronicles 5:1–2). The birthright was taken from Reuben and given to Joseph, the firstborn son of Jacob's wife Rachel.

In its early days, Israel was divided—Judah being the smaller group, and the larger was called Israel: "And Joab gave up the sum of the number of the people unto the king: and there were in Israel eight hundred thousand valiant men that drew the sword; and the men of Judah were five hundred thousand men" (2 Samuel 24:9).

"And the Lord said, I will remove Judah also out of my sight, as I have removed Israel, and will cast off this city Jerusalem which I have chosen, and the house of which I said, My name shall be there" (2 Kings 23:27).

With Ephraim, the covenant son of Joseph (see Genesis 48:1–20), as their leader, Israel was taken into the north at the time the kingdom was overthrown by the Assyrians, about 721 BC. They never returned. According to the prophet Amos, the Lord said that he would sift (scatter) them among all the nations: "I will destroy it from off the face of the earth; saving that I will not utterly destroy the house of Jacob, saith the Lord.

"For, lo, I will command, and I will sift the house of Israel among all nations, like as corn is sifted in a sieve, yet shall not the least grain fall upon the earth" (Amos 9:8–9).

Then the Lord also promised after the sifting (at some future time), he would gather Israel together again: "And I will bring again the captivity of my people of Israel, and they shall build the waste cities, and inhabit them; and they shall plant vineyards, and drink the wine thereof; they shall also make gardens, and eat the fruit of them.

"And I will plant them upon their land, and they shall no more be pulled up out of their land which I have given them, saith the Lord thy God" (Amos 9:14–15).

This latter-day gathering of Israel is just another part of the "marvellous work and a wonder" that God spoke of.

Let's take a look at the blessing pronounced by Moses upon Israel (see Deuteronomy 33). As this relates to Joseph, pay particular attention to his blessing as compared with that of his brothers.

> And of Joseph he said, *Blessed of the Lord be his land*, for the precious things of heaven, for the dew, and for the deep that coucheth beneath,
>
> And for the precious fruits brought forth by the sun, and for the precious things put forth by the moon,
>
> And for the chief things of the ancient mountains, and for the precious things of the lasting hills,
>
> And for the precious things of the earth and fullness thereof, and for the good will of him that dwelt in the bush: let the blessing come upon the head of Joseph, and upon the top of the head of him that was separated from his brethren.
>
> His glory is like the firstling of his bullock, and his horns are like the horns of unicorns: *with them he shall push the people together to the ends of the earth:*

and they are the ten thousands of Ephraim, and they are
the thousands of Manasseh. (Deuteronomy 33:13–17;
italics added)

This was a prophetic patriarchal blessing that was bestowed upon Joseph's house. It refers to a land that would be given to Joseph which would be blessed above all other lands of the Lord. This would be a land of abundance, a choice land above all other lands. The land Moses described was a land of "precious things of the earth and fullness thereof." Where on earth is there such a land as this? Where could that be?

Moses also pointed out that this would be a land where Joseph's seed would have the power and authority in which "he shall push the people together to the ends of the earth: and they are the ten thousands of Ephraim, and they are the thousands of Manasseh," referring to a gathering place of all the peoples of the earth. Too, it refers to the gathering of Israel, who had been "scattered" among the nations (see Deuteronomy 30:3).

Now let's look at the blessing that was given to Joseph by his father Jacob (Israel). Prior to his death, Jacob called his sons together and gave each a blessing (see Genesis 49:1–2). This was his blessing to Joseph;

Joseph is a fruitful bough, even a fruitful bough by a
well; whose branches run over the wall:
The archers have sorely grieved him, and shot at
him, and hated him:
But his bow abode in strength, and the arms of his
hands were made strong by the hands of the mighty
God of Jacob; (from thence is the shepherd, the stone
of Israel:)
Even by the God of thy father, who shall help

thee; and by the Almighty, who shall bless thee with blessings of heaven above, blessings of the deep that lieth under, blessings of the breasts, and of the womb:

The blessings of thy father have prevailed above the blessings of my progenitors unto the utmost bound of the everlasting hills: they shall be on the head of Joseph, and on the crown of the head of him that was separate from his brethren. (Genesis 49:22–26)

Anciently, the prophets wrote and spoke using simile, which is a figure of speech comparing two unlike things, often using the words *like* or *as*. Although Jacob used neither word, they are implied: "Joseph is [like] a fruitful bough by a well; whose branches run over the wall." That is to say the descendents of Joseph would be so numerous they couldn't be contained. They would "run over the wall," over the waters of the ocean, and into a new and "promised" land. This prophecy was realized when Lehi, a prophet in the days of Jeremiah, was warned to take his family and leave Jerusalem before its impending destruction. Lehi was a descendant of Joseph; therefore, Lehi and his descendants were Jews by citizenship, not by lineage. The first book of the Book of Mormon (1 Nephi) describes the story of Lehi and how he brought his family to what we now know as the Americas, thus fulfilling the prophecy of Joseph being like a "fruitful bough by a well whose branches run over the wall" and the receipt of the abundant land that had been promised to Joseph and his seed.

Along with these blessings, we also need to consider the meaning of Joseph's dreams as given in Genesis 37.

And Joseph dreamed a dream, and he told it his

brethren: and they hated him yet the more.

And he said unto them, Hear, I pray you, this dream which I have dreamed:

For, behold, we were binding sheaves in the field, and, lo, my sheaf arose, and also stood upright; and, behold, your sheaves stood round about, and made obeisance to my sheaf.

And his brethren said to him, Shalt thou indeed reign over us? or shalt thou indeed have dominion over us? And they hated him yet the more for his dreams, and for his words.

And he dreamed yet another dream, and told it his brethren, and said, Behold, I have dreamed a dream more; and, behold, the sun and the moon and the eleven stars made obeisance to me.

And he told it to his father, and to his brethren: and his father rebuked him, and said unto him, What is this dream that thou hast dreamed? Shall I and thy mother and thy brethren indeed come to bow down ourselves to thee to the earth? (Genesis 37:5–10)

Not only would this prophesy come to pass on a temporal level when Joseph's family went to Egypt to escape the famine, but it would also come to pass on an eternal level in the last dispensation. To Joseph the blessing of the gathering of Israel was given, and it would be realized through his son Ephraim, the birthright tribe (see Genesis 48). This blessing included the responsibility of bringing to pass the restoration of all things. Once the Gospel was fully restored and once all Israel was restored, they would bow down in eternal gratitude to Joseph (Ephraim) and make "obeisance" to him.

So does it make any sense that God would make greater

promises to Joseph and his descendants—compared to the sons of Jacob—and provide no record of the fulfillment of those promises?

The Lord did indeed make certain that a record should be kept as it pertained to His promises to Joseph and his people. God clearly explained to Ezekiel what He would do.

> The word of the Lord came again unto me, saying, Moreover, thou son of man, take thee one stick, and write upon it, For Judah, and for the children of Israel his companions: then take another stick, and write upon it, For Joseph, the stick of Ephraim, and for all the house of Israel his companions:
>
> And join them one to another into one stick; and they shall become one in thine hand.
>
> And when the children of thy people shall speak unto thee, saying, Wilt thou not shew us what thou meanest by these?
>
> Say unto them, Thus saith the Lord God, Behold, I will take the stick of Joseph, which is in the hand of Ephraim, and the tribes of Israel his fellows, and will put them with him, even with the stick of Judah, and make them one stick, and they shall be one in mine hand." (Ezekiel 37:15–19)

In antiquity, it was a common practice to write on parchment and roll it around a stick. Also, in certain lands it was common to use a stylus for writing on clay tablets that had frames of wood. Whatever the recording medium, that's not important, the symbolism is the same. It is evident that the commandment was given to keep two individual records, each dealing with the history of the two tribes: the Bible for the tribe of Judah and the Book of Mormon for the tribe of Joseph. It only makes sense that the record of Joseph's people would be kept in another land since Joseph was to be "separate from his brethren."

Referring to Ezekiel 37:18, God said that at some future time the people would ask, referring to His words, "What do you mean by these things?" Then, He would cause the stick (record) of one to be combined with the stick (record) of the other "and make them one stick...in my hand." What would be God's purpose in such a thing as combining two books into one? The Lord declared that by the "mouth of two or three witnesses every word may be established" (Matthew 18:16; 2 Corinthians 13:1). The Book of Mormon is "Another Testament of Jesus Christ." It establishes the truth and divinity of the Bible. It testifies of Jesus Christ.

There are those who protest the Book of Mormon, saying the scriptures are complete and there is no need for anything more than that contained in the Bible. To support their claim, these individuals usually quote John, the Revelator:

"For I testify unto every man that heareth the words of the prophecy of this book, If any man shall add unto these things, God shall add unto him the plagues that are written in this book:

"And if any man shall take away from the words of *the book of this prophecy*, God shall take away his part out of the book of life, and out of the holy city, and from the things which are written in this book" (Revelation 22:18–19; italics added).

Plainly put, such a claim is totally flawed. Biblical scholars—Mormons and non-Mormons alike—agree that the exact date as to when the Book of Revelation was written is unknown. They place the date somewhere between AD 64 and 96. At no time between those dates were the books of the New Testament compiled as we have them now, nor would they be for hundreds of years. It is clear that John wrote this warning against adding to or taking from "the book of this prophecy," meaning the book he had written—the Book of Revelation.

Taking this one step further, if John were referring to the current Bible entirely, then he, too, would be in trouble because Moses wrote two similar warnings from God in the Book of Deuteronomy:

"Ye shall not add unto the word which I command you, neither shall ye diminish ought from it, that ye may keep the commandments of the Lord your God which I command you" (Deuteronomy 4:2); and

"What thing soever I command you, observe to do it: thou shalt not add thereto, nor diminish from it" (Deuteronomy 12:32).

So once again, by using some basic reasoning, by familiarizing ourselves with the facts, and putting things in their proper context, we can clearly see that the bottom line is John's statement wasn't referring to the Bible.

Is the Book of Mormon true? Either it is or it isn't. There are millions of sincere devout people who, with all their heart and mind, say it is true.

The problem seems to rest with nonbelievers. Just as millions believe it is true, I dare say there are hundreds of millions who say it isn't true. Not only do they disbelieve, but they also oppose it and openly and vehemently fight against the Book of Mormon. Why? What is it about this book, whose contents are uplifting and edifying and expound the good things of God and His Son Jesus Christ, that would provoke men to anger and violence?

Many are of the opinion that the violence directed toward the Book of Mormon is evidence of its divinity. If the book weren't of God, Satan would simply ignore it and not bother with it. Is there any other book on earth that so many people contend against than the Book of Mormon?

Those who oppose the Book of Mormon also oppose the prophet who translated it, Joseph Smith. Either Joseph was a prophet of God or he wasn't. No other founder of any church is opposed as is Joseph Smith. Those who oppose Joseph Smith are in the same situation as those who opposed and martyred the prophets (including Christ) anciently. For some reason, they feel backed into a corner. They rail against all that has been revealed and restored through Joseph Smith rather than consider their systems of religion may be incomplete.

The latter-day apostle James E. Talmage (1862–1933) tells a story of when he was a young student. He was approached by a man selling oil lamps. James was perfectly happy with the lamp he had, but he was willing to allow the salesman to demonstrate his lamp.

"We entered my room, and I put a match to my well-trimmed lamp. My visitor was high in his praise. It was the best lamp of its kind, he said, and he had never seen a lamp in better trim. He turned the wick up and down, and pronounced the judgment perfect.

"'Now,' he said, 'with your permission I'll light my lamp,' taking it from his satchel. Its light made bright the remotest corner of my room. Its brilliant blaze made the flame in my lamp weak and pale. Until that moment of convincing demonstration, I had never known the dim obscurity in which I had lived and labored, studied and struggled."

James wound up buying the lamp. He told this story as an analogy of sharing the restored Gospel with others. "The man who would sell a lamp," he said, "did not disparage mine. He placed his greater light alongside my feebler flame, and I hasted to obtain it."

It is the mission of The Church of Jesus Christ of Latter-day Saints "not to assail nor ridicule the beliefs of men, but to set before the world a superior light" adding to the light they already have (Albert L. Zobell Jr., *Story Gems* [1953], p. 45–48). They can accept it or reject it. The choice is theirs.

Priesthood Restoration

*W*hat is priesthood? Simply put, priesthood is the power and authority of God delegated to man to act in His name in all things for the salvation of mankind.

It's a fact that a man must be called of God and authorized by the Lord to preach the Gospel and administer in its ordinances. Just as a man cannot resurrect himself, he cannot call himself to the ministry. No ordinance that is performed by one without proper authority, no matter how well intentioned, is valid in God's eyes. "What a hateful thing to say! What's wrong with Mormons?"

Consider what Paul said in regard to acting in a ministerial capacity:

"And no man taketh this honour unto himself, but he that is called of God, as was Aaron.

"So also Christ glorified not himself to be made an high priest; but he that said unto him, Thou art my Son, to day have I begotten thee" (Hebrews 5:4–5).

Even Jesus Christ didn't call himself. He didn't have the authority to do so. He was called of God, his Father, to be the Redeemer of the world.

Authority works no differently here, on earth, than it does in heaven. Look at it this way:

You're walking down the street on your way to the store. You look down, there lying on the sidewalk is someone's checkbook. You open it to see who it belongs to. It just so happens that this is the checkbook of the wealthiest member of your community.

As you're headed to his bank to return his checkbook, a young mother approaches you. She carries one small child on her hip, and from the looks of her abdominal profile, she's well on the way to delivering another. She shares with you a gut-wrenching story of hardship, ill health, and bad luck, all through no fault of her own. The baby is hungry, and the mother needs medical attention.

You look into her sad eyes welling with tears of desperation. The infant looks up at you and pouts. Your heart melts. You want to help her and the baby, but your own finances are strained as it is. Then it hits you! You reach into your hip pocket and pull out the checkbook you found earlier. Taking your pen you write a generous check payable to cash and sign it. You tear it out of the book and hand it to the needy mother. She thanks you profusely as she goes her way and you go yours. You're feeling pretty good. You've ministered to the needy, you've rendered Christlike service by relieving the suffering of two of God's children, you did a good thing!

But wait a minute. What do you think will happen when the mother tries to cash that check? When the bank sees your signature on the check instead of the signature of the rightful owner of the account—the one who has the authority to write checks on that account—what do you think the bank will do? Why will they do that? Exactly, because you didn't have the authority to do so.

Just as we cannot take it upon ourselves to write checks on other people's checking accounts, no matter how good our intentions may be, it is no different when we attempt to take upon us the authority to act in God's name when it comes to administering His Gospel.

However, there is an alternative that is available, but it must be given by the owner of the account. It's known as *power of attorney*. This is the authorization to act on someone else's behalf in legal or business matters. It's no different with God. The priesthood is the authorization to act in His behalf in legal and business matters as they pertain to His plan of salvation.

Some time after Joseph Smith had received the golden plates from the angel Moroni, he was joined by another young man named Oliver Cowdery, a schoolteacher. Oliver would serve as Joseph's scribe during the translation process.

It was the fifteenth day of May 1829, while translating the plates that Joseph and Oliver came across a passage pertaining to baptism and the remission of sins. Having questions about this specific doctrine, they went into the woods to pray and seek further light and knowledge from God. As they prayed,

> A messenger from heaven descended in a cloud of light, and having laid his hands upon us, he ordained us, saying:
>
> Upon you my fellow servants, in the name of Messiah, I confer the Priesthood of Aaron, which holds the keys of the ministering of angels, and of the gospel of repentance, and of baptism by immersion for the remission of sins; and this shall never be taken again from the earth until the sons of Levi do offer again an offering unto the Lord in righteousness.
>
> He said this Aaronic Priesthood had not the power of laying on hands for the gift of the Holy Ghost, but that this should be conferred on us hereafter; and he

commanded us to go and be baptized, and gave us directions that I should baptize Oliver Cowdery, and that afterwards he should baptize me.

Accordingly, we went and were baptized. I baptized him first, and afterwards he baptized me—after which I laid my hands upon his head and ordained him to the Aaronic Priesthood, and afterwards he laid his hands on me and ordained me to the same Priesthood—for so we were commanded.

The messenger who visited us on this occasion and conferred this Priesthood upon us, said that his name was John, the same that is called John the Baptist in the New Testament, and that he acted under the direction of Peter, James and John, who held the keys of the Priesthood of Melchizedek, which Priesthood, he said, would in due time be conferred on us. (JSH 1:68–72)

This remarkable visit from the resurrected prophet John the Baptist restored to the earth additional eternal truths. To administer in the ordinances of the Gospel, such as baptism, one must be ordained to the necessary priesthood (authority) by one holding that same priesthood (authority). The Aaronic Priesthood holds the keys to (1) the ministry of angels, (2) the gospel of repentance, (3) baptism by immersion for the remission of sins. Finally, this priesthood "shall never be taken again from the earth until the sons of Levi do offer again an offering unto the Lord in righteousness." Although this priesthood comes from God, it is limited in that it "had not the power of laying on hands for the gift of the Holy Ghost," and that authority would be received "under the direction of Peter, James and John, who held the keys of the Priesthood of Melchizedek."

Now let's take a moment here to step aside from discussing priesthood authority and consider a few things.

If this were all a figment of Joseph's imagination, if all this were made up, why, or more importantly how, was Joseph able to get into so much detail? Where did these details come from? How was he able to determine that the restoration of the Aaronic Priesthood was necessary and that it could only come through John the Baptist? Why did he use the name "Messiah" instead of Jesus or Jesus Christ? How did he decide which keys the Aaronic Priesthood held and which were held by the Melchizedek Priesthood? Why were Peter, James, and John to deliver those keys and not some other persons? Why not Jesus himself? Why did he throw in the comment regarding the priesthood never being taken away until "the sons of Levi do offer again an offering unto the Lord in righteousness"? If Joseph (and Oliver) had questions about something as basic and fundamental as baptism, where did the Levites offering sacrifice come from? Think about it.

These two priesthoods are a very important part of the "restitution of all things." In order for the final chapter of God's plan to be carried out, these two critical elements (priesthoods) had to be restored. Attempting to restore the full Gospel without the priesthood would be like trying to start a car without a battery.

Shortly after their experience with John the Baptist, Peter, James, and John (the same that were with the Christ during his mortal ministry) came to Joseph and Oliver and conferred upon them the Melchizedek Priesthood. With this came the keys and authority to organize the kingdom of God upon the earth (the Church) in this, the last dispensation.

With the proper and full priesthood restored to the earth once more, the church, as Jesus had established it, could be restored once again. With a grand total of six members, the Church of Jesus Christ was organized. It was April 6, 1830. It wasn't until 1838 that the name The Church of Jesus Christ of Latter-day Saints was made the official name.

You may wonder, "Where did that name come from?" The name was given by the Lord to Joseph through revelation: "For thus shall my church be called in the last days, even The Church of Jesus Christ of Latter-day Saints" (Doctrine and Covenants 115:4).

"Where do you people get off referring to yourselves as 'saints'? What's wrong with Mormons?" There's really no reason to take offense. In the biblical sense of the word, it's simply a title referring to those members of the Church that have been cleansed through baptism and are pure and clean before the Lord. The Apostle Paul, throughout his writings, constantly referred to the members of the various branches of the church as saints. The term is used a total of ninety-five times in the Bible: sixty-one times in the New Testament and thirty-four times in the Old Testament. Here are some examples.

> And it came to pass, as Peter passed throughout all quarters, he came down also to the saints which dwelt at Lydda. (Acts 9:32)

> To all that be in Rome, beloved of God, called to be saints: Grace to you and peace from God our Father, and the Lord Jesus Christ. (Romans 1:7)

> Unto the church of God which is at Corinth, to them that are sanctified in Christ Jesus, called to be saints, with all that in every place call upon the name of Jesus Christ our Lord, both theirs and ours. (1 Corinthians 1:2)

Paul, an apostle of Jesus Christ by the will of God, to the saints which are at Ephesus, and to the faithful in Christ Jesus. (Ephesians 1:1)

He will keep the feet of his saints, and the wicked shall be silent in darkness; for by strength shall no man prevail. (1 Samuel 2:9)

Now therefore arise, O Lord God, into thy resting place, thou, and the ark of thy strength: let thy priests, O Lord God, be clothed with salvation, and let thy saints rejoice in goodness. (2 Chronicles 6:41)

Until the Ancient of days came, and judgment was given to the saints of the most High; and the time came that the saints possessed the kingdom. (Daniel 7:22)

Getting back to the priesthood, the question might be asked, "By what priesthood do the other churches operate?" Because of the apostasy, there was no priesthood upon the earth at the time of the Reformation. There was no authority, there were no keys, nor did anyone or any group claim to hold such power.

The prophets and apostles anciently held these keys (priesthood). When Jesus "called unto him his twelve disciples, he gave them *power* against unclean spirits, to cast them out, and to heal all manner of sickness and all manner of disease" (Matthew 10:1; italics added). And he reminded them, "Ye have not chosen me, but I have chosen you, and ordained you" (John 15:16). They were ordained to the priesthood and given power and authority by him whose it was, he having received it from his Father.

To Peter the Lord promised, "I will give unto thee the *keys* of the kingdom of heaven," meaning that he would have the presiding authority over the church as the chief apostle and prophet. As a result of such power and authority, the Lord told Peter, "Whatsoever thou shalt bind on earth shall be bound in heaven: and whatsoever thou shalt loose on earth shall be loosed in heaven" (Matthew 16:19; italics added). With that power and authority (priesthood keys), Peter had all that was necessary to preach the Gospel and perform the saving ordinances that lead to eternal life.

At this point, a basic understanding of the two priesthoods would be helpful to better understand the Gospel of Jesus Christ and the Church he restored here on earth.

The Aaronic Priesthood, also known as the Levitical Priesthood and sometimes referred to as the Lesser Priesthood, is the priesthood that was given to Aaron and his sons to carry out the work of the preparatory gospel and the carnal laws under which the Israelites had been placed. Therefore, the Aaronic Priesthood is also referred to as the "preparatory priesthood." This priesthood was usually conferred upon the men of the house of Levi who were between thirty and fifty years old (see Numbers 3:4). They served in the temple carrying out those ancient ordinances. Many of their duties were comparable to those of bishops and priests in the Church today. All the ordained Levites held the fullness of the Aaronic Priesthood (see Hebrew 7:5) and participated in the offering of sacrifices. However, they didn't hold the keys of the Aaronic ministry, so many of their duties were comparable to those of teachers and deacons in the Church today.

The Mosaic Law was the "schoolmaster" (see Galatians 3:24) to lead the people to Christ. Its teachings and ordinances were administered by the Aaronic Priesthood. Paul pointed out that perfection couldn't be attained by this priesthood alone. In his letter to the Hebrews, he taught,

> If therefore perfection were by the Levitical priesthood, (for under it the people received the law,) what further need was there that another priest should rise after the order of Melchisedec, and not be called after the order of Aaron?
>
> For the priesthood being changed, there is made of necessity a change also of the law...
>
> For it is evident that our Lord sprang out of Juda; of which tribe Moses spake nothing concerning priesthood...
>
> For he testifieth, Thou art a priest for ever after the order of Melchisedec...
>
> But this man, because he continueth ever, hath an unchangeable priesthood. (Hebrews 7:11–12, 14, 17, and 24)

So it was necessary for God to send another priesthood. Therefore, when Christ replaced the lesser law with the full Gospel, there was also the necessity to provide the higher priesthood which administered it.

John the Baptist was the last in the Levite lineage to hold the Aaronic Priesthood. It was by this authority that he was able to administer the ordinance of baptism by immersion for the remission of sins. However, he didn't have the authority to bestow the gift of the Holy Ghost by the laying on of hands. He made it clear through his teachings that one mightier than he would come, saying, "He shall baptize you with the Holy Ghost" (Matthew 3:11), as we read above in Joseph's account of the Baptist's appearance to him and Oliver as it pertained to their ordination to the Aaronic Priesthood.

The Melchizedek Priesthood, the "greater priesthood," includes the Aaronic Priesthood. It holds the highest authority, which pertains to the priesthood. It holds all the keys of the kingdom of God in all ages. It's the channel through which all knowledge, doctrine, the plan of salvation, and every other important matter is revealed from God.

Regarding the priesthood, God revealed the following to Joseph Smith:

> There are, in the church, two priesthoods, namely, the Melchizedek and Aaronic, including the Levitical Priesthood.
>
> Why the first is called the Melchizedek Priesthood is because Melchizedek was such a great high priest.
>
> Before his day it was called the Holy Priesthood, after the Order of the Son of God.
>
> But out of respect or reverence to the name of the Supreme Being, to avoid the too frequent repetition of his name, they, the church, in ancient days, called that priesthood after Melchizedek, or the Melchizedek Priesthood.
>
> All other authorities or offices in the church are appendages to this priesthood.
>
> But there are two divisions or grand heads—one is the Melchizedek Priesthood, and the other is the Aaronic or Levitical Priesthood.
>
> The Melchizedek Priesthood holds the right of presidency, and has power and authority over all the offices in the church in all ages of the world, to administer in spiritual things. (Doctrine and Covenants 107:1–6, 8)

In order for one to carry out the work of the plan of salvation, having been found worthy, he must be called and ordained by one who already holds those keys.

When Jesus set up his church during his mortal ministry, he being a high priest forever after the order of Melchizedek (see Hebrew 2:17–18; 3:1; 5:6, 10; 6:20; 7:15–17, 21), this holy priesthood was again given to those who were to assist in the work. (See John 15:16; 1 Peter 2:5, 9.) All the apostles held this priesthood. With the death of the apostles there was no one left holding the keys to authorize a person to be ordained to any priesthood office. It was in this way the Lord took the priesthood from the earth because of the wickedness of men.

In order for one to carry out the work of the plan of salvation, having been found worthy, he must be called and ordained by one who already holds those keys. As was said above, the individual cannot assume to take this authority upon himself.

> For every high priest taken from among men is ordained for men in things pertaining to God, that he may offer both gifts and sacrifices for sins.
>
> And no man taketh this honour unto himself, but he that is called of God, as was Aaron.
>
> So also Christ glorified not himself to be made an high priest; but he that said unto him, Thou art my Son, to day have I begotten thee.
>
> As he saith also in another place, Thou art a priest

for ever after the order of Melchisedec (Hebrews 5:1,
4–6).

What could be plainer? "Okay, how was Aaron ordained?"
you ask. The Lord said, speaking to Moses, one who had been
called and ordained already:

"And take thou unto thee Aaron thy brother, and his sons
with him, from among the children of Israel, that he may
minister unto me in the priest's office...

"And thou shalt put [coats, girdles, and bonnets] upon
Aaron thy brother, and his sons with him; and shalt anoint
them, and consecrate them, and sanctify them, that they may
minister unto me in the priest's office" (Exodus 28:1 and 41;
see Exodus 40:12–15).

It was no different with the apostles of the Lord. They didn't
call and ordain themselves:

"And he ordained twelve, that they should be with him, and
that he might send them forth to preach,

"And to have power to heal sicknesses, and to cast out
devils" (Mark 3:14–15).

Let's look at the calling and ordination of Saul, who was
to be known as Paul. His situation provides a clear example of
the order in which such things are done under the direction of
the Lord.

And as he [Saul] journeyed, he came near Damascus:
and suddenly there shined round about him a light
from heaven:

And he fell to the earth, and heard a voice saying
unto him, Saul, Saul, why persecutest thou me?

And he said, Who art thou, Lord? And the Lord
said, I am Jesus whom thou persecutest: it is hard for
thee to kick against the pricks.

And he trembling and astonished said, Lord, what wilt thou have me to do? And the Lord said unto him, Arise, and go into the city, and it shall be told thee what thou must do. (Acts 9:3–6)

Although Jesus spoke to Saul directly, that alone didn't qualify him to the ministry or administration of the ordinances. First, he had to regain his sight. Second, he had to repent of his sins and be baptized. This was all done by Ananias, one who held the priesthood authority to carry out that ordinance. However, it wasn't a simple matter of Saul going into town and telling Ananias what had happened and what he needed done. That's not the way it works, either. The Lord revealed to Ananias his will concerning Saul:

And there was a certain disciple at Damascus, named Ananias; and to him said the Lord in a vision, Ananias. And he said, Behold, I am here, Lord.

And the Lord said unto him, Arise, and go into the street which is called Straight, and enquire in the house of Judas for one called Saul, of Tarsus: for, behold, he prayeth,

And hath seen in a vision a man named Ananias coming in, and putting his hand on him, that he might receive his sight.

And the Lord said unto him, Go thy way: for he is a chosen vessel unto me, to bear my name before the Gentiles, and kings, and the children of Israel. (Acts 9:10–12; 15)

We see here how Ananias received his information about Saul. It came through direct revelation from God through the Holy Ghost. We also see that he was directed by the Lord to

(1) heal Saul of his blindness, by the laying on of hands; (2) to baptize him for a remission of his sins; and (3) give him the gift of the Holy Ghost, which is also given by the laying on of hands (see Acts 8:17; 9:6). None of this could have been accomplished had Ananias not held the Melchizedek priesthood.

What does Saul do next? He bears witness—he testifies—of his conversion experience to all who will listen. Don't mistake bearing one's testimony of the truth for teaching or preaching. They aren't the same.

Saul was well known as one of the Christian persecutors (see Acts 9:1–2). When this same man went around testifying of the truth and reality of Jesus Christ, many of the Christians were leery to say the least, and understandably so, considering his history.

While in Jerusalem, one of the disciples (a member of the church) named Barnabas heard Saul bearing his testimony in the synagogue and was impressed. He took Saul to Antioch:

"Now there were in the church that was at Antioch certain prophets and teachers; as Barnabas...and Saul.

"As they ministered to the Lord, and fasted, the Holy Ghost said, 'Separate me Barnabas and Saul for the work whereunto I have called them.'

"And when they had fasted and prayed, and laid their hands on them, they sent them away" (Acts 13:1–3).

Here we learn some basic truths on the operations of how men are called of God. First, we learn that there were prophets (plural) and teachers (plural) in Antioch whom God had already chosen and set in place. There always has been and always will be prophets and teachers in Christ's church. Second, we see that those who have been chosen to carry out the Lord's work continually seek his will by humbling themselves through fasting and prayer. Third, the Lord then reveals his will through the

Holy Ghost—Spirit speaking to spirit—to those legal ministers who are directing his affairs. In this case, the words spoken to them by the Holy Ghost are of great interest to us, or should be, as to what they teach. He said to them, "Separate me Barnabas and Saul for the work whereunto I have called them." This is what we refer to as being set apart. According to Merriam-Webster Online, to *separate* something, or someone, means "to set or keep apart" and "to make a distinction between." And this is exactly what happens when one is ordained to the work in any capacity, from prophet to teacher. In this instance, Barnabas and Saul were separated or set apart from all other members of the church to the stand apostles—special witnesses—of the Lord Jesus Christ. Fourth, we see that the setting apart is done by the laying of hands. This is an ordinance. In this ordinance, the one having authority lays his hands on the head of the individual who had been called and sets him apart to the specific calling and bestows upon that individual the power and authority (priesthood) necessary to carry out that calling.

How do we know they were called to be apostles? From here on, Luke, the author of the Book of Acts, refers to them as apostles. This indicates they had been set apart as members of the Quorum of the Twelve. That, in turn, indicates that one or more of the other apostles would have to have been present in order to ordain them, confer the priesthood keys upon them, and set them apart to that office. So we see that Saul and Barnabas were sent forth as legal administrators of the Gospel, called by revelation, and authorized to serve in that capacity by the laying on of hands by the Lord's anointed. Therefore, we see the pattern set by the Lord for those chosen to the ministerial service in all ages. If God is consistent and unchanging, then it cannot be otherwise!

Due to the nature and the magnitude of the work in the

plan of salvation, God has divided the priesthood into many subdivisions or offices to carry out the various required duties. Those offices are

Aaronic Priesthood
1. Deacon
2. Teacher
3. Priest
4. Bishop

Melchizedek Priesthood
1. Elder
2. Seventy
3. High priest
4. Patriarch (or evangelist)
5. Apostle
6. Prophet

Each of these offices is mentioned in the New Testament as they pertained to Christ's church (see Luke 10:1; Acts 14:23; Ephesians 1:20; 4:11; 1 Timothy 31:1, 10; 1 Peter 5:1). Granted, some Christian churches today use a few of these titles, but not all are present in all churches, neither are their duties and responsibilities available in the Bible alone, and as unfortunate as it is, they lack the authority to act in these offices. Only through revelation and the restitution of all things has this been made available in this last dispensation.

The Apostle Paul, speaking of the unity of the church, was well aware of the importance of a complete organization when he taught,

And he gave some, apostles; and some, prophets; and some, evangelists; and some, pastors and teachers;

For the perfecting of the saints, for the work of

the ministry, for the edifying of the body of Christ:

Till we all come in the unity of the faith, and of the knowledge of the Son of God, unto a perfect man, unto the measure of the stature of the fulness of Christ:

That we henceforth be no more children, tossed to and fro, and carried about with every wind of doctrine, by the sleight of men, and cunning craftiness, whereby they lie in wait to deceive. (Ephesians 4:11–14)

With the advent of the Great Apostasy, the world has indeed been "tossed to and fro, and carried about with every wind of doctrine, by the sleight of men and cunning craftiness." With the proper organization of the church having been abandoned and with the loss of priesthood and its keys, powers, and authority, what else could be expected?

Had it not been for the promised restoration, had it not been for the return of revelation, we wouldn't have these truths and these tools available to us today.

Where Did I Come From?

*B*ack in chapter 1, I had mentioned three questions that often weighed heavily upon me, from time to time. Those questions were

> Where did I come from?
>
> Why am I here?
>
> Where am I going after I die?

Many people have voiced these questions, perhaps using different words, but the basic inquiry was still the same. Long before I ever bumped into Linda, I had asked different people what their thoughts were in these regards. Some were philosophy teachers in college, some were ministers from various churches, some were friends, and some were family. None of them had a direct, concise answer to any of these questions. And of all the answers I was given, no two were ever alike.

Growing up through my teenage years, and well into young adulthood, I often toyed with the idea of going into the ministry. After all, I came from a very religious family. My family attended Sunday school and church worship services every Sunday. My grandfather on my mother's side was a minister. One of mother's brothers was a minister and one of mother's brothers-in-law was a minister. I had a first cousin who was a minister in an ongoing mission in Africa. Yet with all this influence around me and the great desire to serve God, something just didn't seem quite right. It felt as though something was missing.

During the course of my six-week discussion with the Elders, I couldn't help bringing up the first question: *Where did we come from?*

Their answer went something like this, "We are, literally, children of our Heavenly Father. We lived with Him as spirits before we were born on this earth. Each of us was a unique individual."

Right now, someone somewhere is reading this and thinking, "Where in the world do you folks get these crazy ideas? What's wrong with Mormons?"

There was a premortal existence, also referred to as our first estate. To me it felt good, it felt right, it was as though it was something I had known all along but had forgotten somewhere along the way.

No matter what other churches may teach, there are those whose spirits are more susceptible to the things of God even though they may not have found these eternal truths. One example is found in a poem by William Wordsworth.

> *Our birth is but a sleep and a forgetting:*
> *The soul that rises with us, our life's star,*
> *Hath had elsewhere its setting,*
> *And cometh from afar;*
> *Not in entire forgetfulness,*
> *And not in utter nakedness,*
> *But trailing clouds of glory*
> *Do we come from God*
> *Who is our home.*

(William Wordsworth, "Ode: Intimations of Immortality from Recollections of Early Childhood.")

We dwelt in God's presence. We saw His face. We heard His voice. We knew Him as well then as we know our earthly fathers now. We are the offspring of God: "I have said, 'Ye are gods; and all of you are children of the most High'" (Psalms 82:6).

That being true, it means that each of us—you and I—have a divine spark within us. We have that potential to become like Him (we'll talk more about this shortly).

We've already seen that Jesus (Jehovah) dwelt with God before he was born. We also learned that Lucifer, the devil, "and a third part of the stars of heaven" who followed him, also dwelt with God. These stars were "the angels which kept not their first estate, but left their own habitation, he [God] hath reserved in everlasting chains under darkness unto the judgment of the great day" (Jude 1:6). Angels are nothing more or less than those individuals who dwell in the presence of God. Too, we know that stars, those glowing pinpoints in the night sky, can't and won't follow anyone. The term is simply a metaphor used by the prophetic author for those angels—sons and daughters—that dwelt with God the Eternal Father. They failed to keep, or live up to, their first estate, which strongly implies there is more than one estate to keep. They were cast out of their habitation, or place of dwelling. Therefore, if they weren't living with God at the time, then how else could they be cast out of His presence?

The chief apostle, Peter, clearly understood this great doctrine: "God spared not the angels that sinned, but cast them down to hell, and delivered them into chains of darkness, to be reserved unto judgment" (2 Peter 2:4). Remember, they sinned in that they rebelled and sought to follow Lucifer's plan rather than Heavenly Father's.

In Job 38, God asks him, "Where wast thou when I laid the foundations of the earth? declare, if thou hast understanding.

"When the morning stars sang together, and all the sons of God shouted for joy?" (Job 38:4, 7).

It's clear there were sons (and daughters) with God while

The prophets were appointed in their time and their callings upon the earth prior to their coming here.

He was in the earliest stages of forming the earth. It's clear too that we (those sons and daughters) had an understanding of what He was doing and why. As a result of that understanding, we "sang together" and "shouted for joy" because a place was being prepared for us!

Paul also understood this doctrine and the fact that God did know the spirits of mankind before they came to earth. If not, how could He justly appoint "the bounds of their habitation" on the earth? Consider the following:

"And [God] hath made of one blood all nations of men for to dwell on all the face of the earth, and *hath determined the times before appointed*, and the bounds of their habitation" (Acts 17:26; italics added).

The prophets were appointed in their time and their callings upon the earth prior to their coming here. We see this in the calling of the prophet Jeremiah, who was chosen before he was born:

"Then the word of the Lord came unto me, saying, Before I formed thee in the belly I knew thee; and before thou camest forth out of the womb I sanctified thee, and I ordained thee a prophet unto the nations" (Jeremiah 1:4–5).

Can the concept be stated any plainer? *Before* Jeremiah was conceived in the womb by his father and mother, God *knew* him. *Before* he was born, God sanctified him. *Before* he was born, God ordained him to be a prophet. God selected Jeremiah while he was in his first estate because He knew him and knew what kind of son he was—one He could trust to act justly and righteously in the office of prophet to which he was *fore*ordained, not predestined. Let's take a moment here and explore the difference between the two.

To be *predestined* to something is to imply that no matter what one does, good, bad, or indifferent, the outcome will be the same. That thing, whatever it may be, will come to pass. Nothing could be further from the truth! It totally negates agency—the God-given gift of choice.

To be *foreordained*, as was Jeremiah for example, means he was called and set apart to that calling while yet a spirit, while he was still in his first estate, in the presence of his Heavenly Father. Once he was born, a veil of forgetfulness was drawn over his mind (as is the case for us all) in order that he could move through his life exercising faith. Although one may be foreordained, one still has his agency. In this life, one can—one must—still choose between good and evil, right and wrong, just and unjust. Should one choose unwisely, the promised blessing of the foreordination is made null and void. If this weren't true and if life were predestined, then what is the value of faith?

"What about Saul?" you ask. Good thinking! Saul is an excellent example. Saul, as do many of us, acted upon the knowledge and information he had on hand at the time. Unlike the laws of man, with God ignorance of the law (to a point) *is* an excuse. Once the truth was made known to Saul—once he was shown the error of his ways and a way was provided to repent of those errors—he, using his agency, *chose* to follow another course. He repented of his sins, was baptized for the remission of those sins, received the gift of the Holy Ghost, and moved in a totally new direction, one leading back into the presence of his Heavenly Father. Sadly, not everyone chooses to accept and follow the truth when it's been placed before them. Just look at the Sadducees and the Pharisees as one example.

Getting back to the preexistence, Paul, writing to Titus, one of his missionary companions, stated in his salutation referring to himself as being one who understood: "In hope of eternal life, which God, that cannot lie, promised before the world began" (Titus 1:2).

So Paul understood that God had made certain promises to certain individuals. When? "Before the world began." It seems that all we have in the Bible are pieces of a bigger picture—a greater truth.

This greater truth was revealed to Joseph Smith while translating some of the writings of the prophet Abraham. These records were written while Abraham was in Egypt. The ancient papyri that had come into Joseph's possession had been taken from the catacombs of Egypt. The Lord had revealed to Abraham the truth about our first estate and a grand council that was held there regarding the formation of the earth and the plan of salvation:

> Now the Lord had shown unto me, Abraham, the intelligences that were organized before the world was; and among all these there were many of the noble and great ones;
>
> And God saw these souls that they were good, and he stood in the midst of them, and he said: These I will make my rulers; for he stood among those that were spirits, and he saw that they were good; and he said unto me: Abraham, thou art one of them; thou wast chosen before thou wast born.
>
> And there stood one among them that was like unto God, and he said unto those who were with him: We will go down, for there is space there, and we will take of these materials, and we will make an earth whereon these may dwell;

And we will prove them herewith, to see if they will do all things whatsoever the Lord their God shall command them;

And they who keep their first estate shall be added upon; and they who keep not their first estate shall not have glory in the same kingdom with those who keep their first estate; and they who keep their second estate shall have glory added upon their heads for ever and ever."

And the Lord said: Whom shall I send? And one answered like unto the Son of Man: Here am I, send me. And another answered and said: Here am I, send me. And the Lord said: I will send the first.

And the second was angry, and kept not his first estate; and, at that day, many followed after him. (Abraham 3:22–28)

Thus, we see that the spirits of men and women were in the beginning with God before the foundations of the world were laid. There the plan of salvation was made known to us.

The promise that Paul spoke of to Titus was, "They who keep their first estate shall be added upon." He goes on to explain that "they who keep not their first estate shall not have glory in the same kingdom with those who keep their first estate." And those who elected to follow Lucifer saw that promise fulfilled early on in the process. They failed to keep their first estate.

So it's clear to see from the scriptures that our spirits, as spirit children of God, existed before we were born into mortality. We came from the presence of our Heavenly Father. We were they who "sang together" and "shouted for joy" after hearing the Plan!

Why Am I Here?

*T*he information provided by Abraham leads us into the second question: *Why am I here?*

Contrary to popular belief, this life has a purpose. This life was provided to give us the opportunity to learn and to grow. God the Father has proclaimed, "This is my work and my glory—to bring to pass the immortality and eternal life of man" (Moses 1:39). His Son, Jesus Christ, commanded, "Be ye therefore perfect, even as your Father which is in heaven is perfect" (Mathew 5:48). That isn't a cruel taunt. It's not asking for the impossible. Would God, through His Son, give us a commandment that was impossible to achieve? I'll grant you, it is, without a doubt, the greatest challenge ever issued to anyone, but it is doable, with Christ's help. It starts at our birth.

Each spirit son and daughter who is born into mortality receives a physical body. Here, our spirits and our bodies are joined together for a time. Our bodies, as we know all too well, are mortal and imperfect. Our mortal bodies are composed of flesh, blood, and spirit. "The life of the flesh is in the blood" (Leviticus. 17:11), meaning that when too much blood is shed, the spirit leaves the body and the individual dies. That dead body then decays and goes back to the dust, or elements, from which it was made. Receiving this body is the first step on that long, long road to becoming *like* our Heavenly Father.

From Adam's fall, we all inherit death; that is, we are all

mortal and we will all die temporally. Through the Atonement of Jesus Christ we all will be resurrected, meaning our bodies and our spirits will be reunited never to die again: "For as in Adam all die, even so in Christ shall all be made alive" (1 Corinthians 15:22). As a result of Adam's transgression, we are also spiritually dead—removed from the presence of our Father and our God: "Wherefore, as by one man sin entered into the world, and death by sin; and so death passed upon all men, for that all have sinned" (Romans 5:12). This is why Adam and Eve were cast out of the Garden. In reality, that was a blessing! "And the Lord God said, 'Behold, the man is become as one of us, to know good and evil'" (Genesis 3:22).

So the process had begun. Adam and Eve and all their descendents, including you and me, had started on the path to "become as one of [them, the Gods], to know good and evil." Receiving a body was the first step. Being exposed to and understanding the difference between good and evil was the second. First, we get a mortal body through birth; second, we get an immortal body through the resurrection. Living in a temporal world with a mortal body provides the ways and the means by which experiences, tests, trials, and tribulations prepare those who are faithful to gain eternal life—returning to the presence of their Heavenly Father.

As was mentioned, one thing we did bring with us was our agency. We had it in the premortal existence. We chose the side of Christ, not Lucifer; and so we are privileged to enter into this, our "second estate." As I said, this is a test. We will be proved to see if we will do whatsoever the Lord commands. This is a probationary state. Here, we are free to choose between good and evil. Like it or not, regardless of what any smooth-talking defense attorney may say, we *are* accountable for our choices. As we move from infancy up through early childhood, we learn right from wrong. Each of us was born with the "light of Christ." This is the means by which we inherently know right from wrong. Some call it the conscience; others call it the Spirit of Christ; others call it the Light of Christ. The Lord told Joseph Smith it is "the true light that lighteth every man that cometh into the world" (Doctrine and Covenants 93:2). In the Book of Mormon, the prophet Mormon stated, "The Spirit of Christ is given to every man, that he may know good from evil" (Moroni 7:16). So with that in mind, and recalling that God is not a respecter of persons, all persons are in the position to believe the truth when it is placed before them. Whether or not they choose to do so is another story.

Agency, the ability to choose, is at the foundation of all progression. It is based on the truth that there must be opposition in all things. If there were no opposites, there would be nothing. The Book of Mormon prophet Lehi explained it this way:

> And because of the intercession for all, all men come unto God; wherefore, they stand in the presence of him, to be judged of him according to the truth and holiness which is in him. Wherefore, the ends of the law which the Holy One hath given, unto the inflicting of the punishment which is affixed, which punishment that is affixed is in opposition to that of the happiness which is affixed, to answer the ends of the atonement—
>
> For it must needs be, that there is an opposition in all things. If not so, my first-born in the wilderness, righteousness could not be brought to pass, neither wickedness, neither holiness nor misery, neither good nor bad. Wherefore, all things must needs be a compound in one; wherefore, if it should be one

body it must needs remain as dead, having no life neither death, nor corruption nor incorruption, happiness nor misery, neither sense nor insensibility.

Wherefore, it must needs have been created for a thing of naught; wherefore there would have been no purpose in the end of its creation. Wherefore, this thing must needs destroy the wisdom of God and his eternal purposes, and also the power, and the mercy, and the justice of God.

And if ye shall say there is no law, ye shall also say there is no sin. If ye shall say there is no sin, ye shall also say there is no righteousness. And if there be no righteousness there be no happiness. And if there be no righteousness nor happiness there be no punishment nor misery. And if these things are not there is no God. And if there is no God we are not, neither the earth; for there could have been no creation of things, neither to act nor to be acted upon; wherefore, all things must have vanished away. (2 Nephi 2:10–13)

Therefore, if we weren't accountable for our own sins, if we're not agents unto ourselves, then the very reason for the creation would disappear and the great plan of salvation would be meaningless.

Lehi goes on to explain that such isn't the case.

And now, my sons, I speak unto you these things for your profit and learning; for there is a God, and he hath created all things, both the heavens and the earth, and all things that in them are, both things to act and things to be acted upon.

And to bring about his eternal purposes in the end of man, after he had created our first parents, and the beasts of the field and the fowls of the air, and in fine, all things which are created, it must needs be that there was an opposition; even the forbidden fruit in opposition to the tree of life; the one being sweet and the other bitter.

Wherefore, the Lord God gave unto man that he should act for himself. Wherefore, man could not act for himself save it should be that he was enticed by the one or the other. (2 Nephi 2:14–16)

This explains why God gave what appeared to be two conflicting commandments to Adam and Eve: to have children and do not eat of the tree of knowledge of good and evil, which would put them in a position to have children. The issue before all of us is choosing between opposites. If they hadn't partaken of the fruit, they would have remained in the Garden and would still be there today, and none of us would have ever been born. The plan of salvation would have been useless, but because of God's infinite wisdom and His omniscience, He knew what would happen, and He prepared a way to overcome the results of the Fall—that is the Atonement of Jesus Christ.

In its most simple form, our purpose for being here is to choose between righteousness and wickedness—Jesus Christ or Satan. Without a proper understanding of this basic concept and how the plan of salvation works, is it any wonder that so many are suffering such deep despair when they struggle with the question, "Why am I here"?

As we move through this life—this probationary state—hopefully we will make the right choices more often than not. Between birth and death, one of the most important choices we can make is the person we choose to marry.

To the best of my knowledge, there is no other church on

the face of the earth that believes in or teaches the marriage contract between a man and a woman extends beyond the grave. However, God said, "It is not good that the man should be alone; I will make him an help meet for him...Therefore shall a man leave his father and his mother, and shall cleave unto his wife: and *they shall be one flesh*" (Genesis 2:18 & 24; italics added).

It's important to remember, it was *before* the Fall of Adam and Eve that God declared, "It is not good that the man should be alone," and that the man and the woman "shall be one flesh." If this were true before the Fall, and since God had made them "one flesh" and in light of their redemption from the Fall, isn't it just as important that this union be in effect after the Fall, considering that they, as resurrected beings, will live forever?

If this weren't so, and if this weren't understood by Christ's apostles, then why did Paul teach: "Nevertheless neither is the man without the woman, neither the woman without the man, in the Lord"? (1 Corinthians 11:11). Since this concept originated with God, it is, by its very nature, a divine, eternal concept. Where else can one learn more about love, temperance, patience, selflessness, godliness, brotherly kindness, self-discipline, and sacrifice than in the sacred institution of marriage? What a training ground it can be! Without the union of the sexes, we cannot become perfect as the Lord has charged us.

Consider the Lord's promise to Peter (and the rest of the twelve): "And I will give unto thee the keys of the kingdom of heaven: and whatsoever thou shalt bind on earth shall be bound in heaven: and whatsoever thou shalt loose on earth shall be loosed in heaven" (Matthew 16:19). Remember, he is speaking of the priesthood power and authority here, and it is by this authority and power that men and women are bound (sealed) together as husband and wife for time *and* eternity.

At the death of whichever spouse dies first, that most sacred partnership is dissolved. They are no longer married; they are no longer husband and wife.

What else would a servant of the Lord be binding on earth that would be bound in heaven? A man and woman—a husband and wife! Speaking of husbands and wives, Jesus taught the Pharisees that once married, the man and woman "are no more twain, *but one flesh*. What therefore God hath joined together, let not man put asunder" (Matthew 19:6; italics added). Yet that is exactly what man has done. At some point during the Great Apostasy, it was recognized that no one held the power and authority to marry a man and woman for time and eternity. It had been taken from the earth. Yet in ceremony after ceremony, ministers read from the above verse, saying, "What therefore God hath joined together, let not man put asunder," and then he immediately turns around and adds a contradictory clause to the contract which states, "until death do you part," because of the absence of priesthood authority to do otherwise. At the death of whichever spouse dies first, that most sacred partnership is dissolved. They are no longer married; they are no longer husband and wife.

Christ will always be the head of the Church. There will never be a time when he is not the head of the Church. It is a permanent relationship, never to be "put asunder." So consider the analogy used by Paul (one who understood this doctrine) when he addressed the saints at Ephesus:

> Wives, submit yourselves unto your own husbands, as unto the Lord.
>
> For the husband is the head of the wife, even as

Christ is the head of the church: and he is the saviour of the body.

Therefore as the church is subject unto Christ, so let the wives be to their own husbands in every thing.

Husbands, love your wives, even as Christ also loved the church, and gave himself for it. (Ephesians 5:22–25)

If Christ will always stand as the head of the Church, and if husbands are to love their wives as Christ loves his Church, then how could such love be set aside at death?

Still in doubt? Okay, when Peter wrote his first Epistle to the Christians in the various provinces of what we now call Asia Minor, he too spoke of the relationship between husbands and wives. Using Sara and Abraham as an example, he said, "Likewise, ye husbands, dwell with them according to knowledge, giving honour unto the wife, as unto the weaker vessel, and as *being heirs together of the grace of life*; that your prayers be not hindered" (1 Peter 3:7; italics added). They are "heirs together" as a couple—as husband and wife—one flesh.

One of you is asking, "What about where Jesus said, 'For in the resurrection they neither marry, nor are given in marriage'?" Okay, let's read the entire passage so as to not take anything out of context.

The same day came to him the Sadducees, *which say that there is no resurrection*, and asked him,

Saying, Master, Moses said, If a man die, having no children, his brother shall marry his wife, and raise up seed unto his brother.

Now there were with us seven brethren: and the first, when he had married a wife, deceased, and, having no issue, left his wife unto his brother:

Likewise the second also, and the third, unto the seventh.

And last of all the woman died also.

Therefore in the resurrection whose wife shall she be of the seven? for they all had her.

Jesus answered and said unto them, Ye do err, not knowing the scriptures, nor the power of God.

For in the resurrection they neither marry, nor are given in marriage, but are as the angels of God in heaven. (Matthew 22:23–30; italics added)

First of all, the Sadducees didn't believe in the resurrection. Secondly, insofar as the resurrection is concerned, there can be no doubt as to whose wife the woman will be from an eternal perspective. All, except for the first marriage, were for time only. Based on Jewish tradition, these other marriages were solely for the purpose of continuing the name and family of the brother who died first.

In relating the same incident, Luke records the Lord's reply this way: "But they which shall be accounted worthy to obtain that world, and the resurrection from the dead, neither marry nor are given in marriage.

"Neither can they die any more: for they are equal unto the angels; and are the children of God, being the children of the resurrection" (Luke 20:35–36).

In the resurrection, there is neither marrying nor giving in marriage. The question of who is married to whom is settled long before then, based on whether or not they were sealed (bound) by the proper priesthood authority while in mortality.

Along these same lines, the Lord revealed to the Prophet Joseph Smith,

Therefore, if a man marry him a wife in the world,

and he marry her not by me nor by my word, and he covenant with her so long as he is in the world and she with him, their covenant and marriage are not of force when they are dead, and when they are out of the world; therefore, they are not bound by any law when they are out of the world.

Therefore, when they are out of the world they neither marry nor are given in marriage; but are appointed angels in heaven, which angels are ministering servants, to minister for those who are worthy of a far more, and an exceeding, and an eternal weight of glory.

For these angels did not abide my law; therefore, they cannot be enlarged, but remain separately and singly, without exaltation, in their saved condition, to all eternity; and from henceforth are not gods, but are angels of God forever and ever. (Doctrine and Covenants 132:15–17)

Perfection cannot be obtained singly or individually. It requires a husband *and* a wife who are sealed to each other. As far as God is concerned, a husband *and* a wife, when married by one having that proper authority to bind for eternity, are one for they are no longer "twain, but one flesh."

Not only are the husband and wife sealed together, but also the children that are born to them while under that covenant are sealed to them as well. It is in this family unit—father, mother, and children—that we learn even more how to become like God.

Do you remember the story I shared with you back in chapter 1 when I asked my mother what would happen to her and me when we died? Well, the doctrine of eternal families answers that question.

It was hard for me then, and it is hard for me now, to believe that God created the kind of love that is had between husbands and wives and parents and children only to have that love torn away by death. It simply doesn't stand to reason. It's true that adult animals no longer recognize their offspring when their young are grown. But the human mother, regardless of how much time has passed, will never forget the child she bore. God, in His infinite wisdom and love, has provided the means by which that love can continue. Families can be together forever.

This reminds me of something I saw on Phil Donahue's television program some years ago. This particular show was looking at people who had died clinically and later resuscitated. There was one woman's story that I thought was especially poignant. If I remember correctly, and I may not, she had died while on the operating table. After she had passed through the tunnel of light, she entered into the presence of those who had already died—the spirit world. At this point in her story she began to tear up, saying, "The one thing that I was keenly aware of, as I walked into the presence of those other spirits, was that I was nobody's wife. I was nobody's mother. I was nobody's daughter. I was nobody's sister." She went on to describe how devastating that felt. How sad it is to think that so many have and will turn away from the God-given opportunity to correct that problem through the restored Church and the priesthood that administers these lifesaving and family-saving ordinances.

We are here to receive a body. We are here to learn how to properly exercise our agency. We are here to learn how to properly repent of our sins. We are here in a probationary state to gain experience; it is a time of testing, an opportunity to prove ourselves and qualify for all that our Heavenly Father has prepared for us to receive.

Where Am I Going After I Die?

"*I*'ve heard that Mormons think they're all going to heaven and everyone else is going to hell. That's an arrogant attitude! What's wrong with Mormons?" That's what the Church's detractors would have you think, but they're wrong.

If God the Father had an eternal plan, wouldn't it stand to reason that His sons and daughters would need to know and understand that plan in order to put it to work effectively? Without that knowledge, religion is lacking and ineffective.

To most Christians, salvation is simply going to heaven as opposed to being damned to hell. For most of them, it's either one or the other. To members of The Church of Jesus Christ of Latter-day Saints, salvation is a process, not just an end.

Salvation and damnation are the opposite ends of a very wide spectrum. Remember, as we discussed, there are opposites in *all* things. Full salvation, also known as exaltation, is to be like God, to be a joint-heir with Jesus Christ, meaning that we receive all that he does, even the fullness of the Father. This is often referred to as eternal life. Full damnation, on the other hand, is to be like Lucifer, to be a joint-heir as it were with the devil, meaning that we receive all that he does, even the fullness of eternal suffering. This is often referred to as eternal damnation.

In between those two extremes lies a vast middle ground. Just as there are varying degrees of behavior, there are varying degrees of salvation and damnation. If one accepts the Gospel in its fullness and lives accordingly, one inherits full salvation. On the other hand, if one were to totally reject and oppose the Gospel, that individual inherits full damnation. In between the two are many varying degrees of salvation. Depending on how much truth of Gospel one accepts and conforms to determines the degree of one's salvation. "In my Father's house are many mansions: if it were not so, I would have told you. I go to prepare a place for you" (John 14:2). So it appears the Lord understood that men believed in degrees of glory in the next life. If this weren't the case, there could be no judgment according to our works. John the Revelator knew this to be true: "And I saw the dead, small and great, stand before God; and the books were opened: and another book was opened, which is the book of life: and the dead were *judged* out of those things which were written in the books, *according to their works*" (Revelation 20:12; italics added). It is self-evident that one man's work will differ from another. Where would the justice be if it were a one-size-fits-all judgment? Also, if there weren't varying degrees or levels of salvation in eternity, the Lord would, in his own words, have told us such was the case.

Paul, in his letter to the Philippians, encouraged them: "Work out your own salvation with fear and trembling" (Philippians 2:12). Think about that for a moment. What does it mean for us to "work out [our] own salvation with fear and trembling"? First of all, it's again obvious that there is more involved in gaining salvation than mere lip service. Next, we learn that salvation is a process that takes time and patience and requires work(s) on our part. But let's not stop there. Reading further, Paul reminds us, "For it is God which worketh in you both to will and to do of his good pleasure" (Philippians 2:13). The works we do are not ours but the

Works are not accomplished through mere lip service alone. Jesus is our example. We are to follow him in every-thing, obviously with the exception of the atonement, but in all other things we are to *do* his works and not be "hearers only" (James 1:22).

Lord's. He works through us to bless others. So we are not doing our own works, but works of the Lord. In preparing his apostles for the looming crucifixion, Jesus declared, "Verily, verily, I say unto you, He that believeth on me, *the works that I do shall he do also; and greater works than these shall he do*; because I go unto my Father" (John 14:12; italics added). Works are not accomplished through mere lip service alone. Jesus is our example. We are to follow him in everything, obviously with the exception of the atonement, but in all other things we are to *do* his works and not be "hearers only" (James 1:22).

Let's take another side street here and talk about works because I know what you're thinking: "We're saved by grace alone through faith in Jesus Christ." Well, that's true, but it's not that simple. We are also saved, in part, by our works. Just as John pointed out, we will be judged by our works. He made that very plain. The best explanation of this doctrine was given by the Apostle James. He starts by saying, "Be ye doers of the word, and not hearers only" (James 1:22). This echoes back to the problem of those who merely pay lip service to the Lord and nothing else—they don't *do* anything that is Christlike in their life to the blessing of others. Think of it this way: if you were arrested for being a Christian, would there be enough evidence to convict you in a court of law?

We've all known people like this somewhere along the way, those that pay lip service only. What they say and what they do are two different things. Benjamin Franklin knew "a good example is the best sermon" (*Poor Richard's Almanac*, p. 141). And didn't Jesus provide the best example? The following illustrates what I'm talking about: James teaches that "if any man among you seem to be religious, and bridleth not his tongue, but deceiveth his own heart, this man's religion is vain" (James 1:26). Wow! That's pretty blunt. The use of profane, vulgar language (a negative work) can cause our religion (faith) to be worthless. Would a true follower of Christ use profane, vulgar language? Many who claim to follow him do!

Speaking of works specifically, James declared,

> Even so *faith, if it hath not works, is dead, being alone.*
>
> Yea, a man may say, Thou hast faith, and I have works: shew me thy faith without thy works, and *I will shew thee my faith by my works.*
>
> Thou believest that there is one God; thou doest well: the devils also believe, and tremble.
>
> But wilt thou know, O vain man, *that faith without works is dead?*
>
> Was not Abraham our father justified by works, when he had offered Isaac his son upon the altar?
>
> Seest thou how faith wrought with his works, and by works was faith made perfect?
>
> And the scripture was fulfilled which saith, Abraham believed God, and it was imputed unto him for righteousness: and he was called the Friend of God.
>
> Ye see then how that *by works a man is justified, and not by faith only.*

Likewise also was not Rahab the harlot justified by works, when she had received the messengers, and had sent them out another way? (See Joshua 2 & 6.)

For as the body without the spirit is dead, so *faith without works is dead also.* (James 2:17–26; italics added)

For one to simply say that he believes in God simply isn't sufficient to attain full salvation. As James said, the devils believe in God, and of what value is that acknowledgment to them? Faith in the Christ—true and proper faith—produces works. These are the works that grow out of faith and justify men before God. (See Matthew 5:16; 16:27; John 14:12.) Faith is the root, and works are the fruit. If our works are good, then our faith is good. Remember, the Lord said corrupt trees cannot bear good fruit.

The works the apostles spoke of in specific cases as being dead were those of the Law of Moses. Those works were replaced with the works of the New Covenant established by Jesus himself.

"Well, wait a minute. What about grace? In Ephesians it says, 'For by grace are ye saved through faith; and that not of yourselves: it is the gift of God.'" That's true, but as we've seen, there's more to it than that. We are saved by grace *after* all we can do. This principle is beautifully illustrated in a short film about a little girl and a bicycle.

The film opens with the little girl dreaming about expertly riding a beautiful new bicycle. The little girl goes and tells her dad and mom that she's had the dream, again. Then she shyly asks her dad, "When can I have a bicycle?"

Her dad looks at her thoughtfully then asks, "Are you willing to earn it?"

"Yes, I'll do anything!" she eagerly replies.

"You work really hard and save your money, and you can have a bicycle," he says.

Then we see a montage of the little girl working at various tasks that are all bigger than she is: working a lemonade stand, working in a garden, struggling to wash an uncooperative dog that probably weighs twice what she does, and mowing the lawn with an old-fashioned, manual push mower.

Eventually, she approaches her dad and asks, "Do you think I have enough money to buy a bike?"

He wisely replies, "I think you've got enough to look at one." (How much money does it take to look?)

"Right now?" she asks excitedly.

"I guess we could go look," he agrees.

At the bicycle shop, the little girl runs inside, pulling her dad behind her, right to the bike she's been dreaming of. "This is the one!" she announces.

She looks at the price tag. The sad realization replaces her excited expression. She's crestfallen. "I'll never have enough to buy a bike, will I, Daddy?"

Her dad tenderly answers, "Well, let's see how much money you've saved."

The little girl reaches deep into her pocket. She pulls out a few crumpled bills and some loose change, and deposits it all in her dad's hand. Just by looking at the meager sum, it's obvious to him that she has fallen way short of having earned enough money to buy the bicycle.

He looks at her solemnly and says, "You don't have enough." She's heartbroken. "But I'll tell what I'll do." She perks up a little. "If you give me all that you have, with a big hug and a kiss, the bike is yours."

It doesn't matter that a person says he believes or has faith in Jesus Christ. What does matter is how the person lives, what he thinks, what he does, even what he says.

Thrilled, the little girl throws her arms around her dad's neck in appreciation and gives him a kiss on the cheek.

The closing shot is the little girl riding the bike home with Dad right behind her.

Each of us is like the little girl. More often than not, what is required of us feels as though it's more than we can handle. The truth of the matter is no matter how hard we try, no matter hard we work, we will come up short of having done enough to merit, of ourselves, entering back into our Heavenly Father's presence. That's where God's grace comes into play. It will be a gift from God, just as the bike was from the dad to the little girl.

So if anyone tries to tell you Mormons don't believe in grace, don't you believe him. The Book of Mormon prophet Nephi declared, "For we know that it is by grace that we are saved, *after* all we can do" (2 Nephi 25:23; italics added). There's that action verb again, "do." Elsewhere in the Book of Mormon, another prophet, Moroni, encourages us to "come unto Christ, and be perfected in him, and deny yourselves of all ungodliness; and if ye shall deny yourselves of all ungodliness, and love God with all your might, mind and strength, *then is his grace sufficient for you*, that by his grace ye may be perfect in Christ" (Moroni 10:32). Just like the dad in the film, God asks his children, "Give me all that you have, and I'll make up the difference."

So you can see that certain things are required: "If ye love me, keep my commandments" (John 14:15). It doesn't matter that a person says he believes or has faith in Jesus Christ. What does matter is how the person lives, what he thinks, what he does, even what he says. Beliefs come from thoughts. Thoughts are expressed in words. The thoughts and words are made visible in deeds—works. The Lord warned:

> Not every one that *saith* unto me, 'Lord, Lord,' shall enter into the kingdom of heaven; but he that *doeth* the will of my Father which is in heaven.
>
> Many will say to me in that day, 'Lord, Lord, have we not prophesied in thy name? and in thy name have cast out devils? and in thy name done many wonderful works?
>
> And then will I profess unto them, 'I never knew you: depart from me, ye that work iniquity' (Matthew 7:21–23; italics added).

Can you imagine hearing the Lord saying that? Why would the Lord cast out those who believe in him? Because they profess to love him with their lips, they profess to receive him with their mouths, but they didn't do the things he commanded them to do. They didn't repent of their sins. They didn't love God with all their heart, might, mind, and strength. They failed to love their neighbor as themselves. They failed to be baptized by one having authority for the remission of sins. They failed to receive the gift of the Holy Ghost by the laying on of hands. They failed to identify themselves with his people. They are not numbered among his chosen ones. "Therefore to him that knoweth to do good, and *doeth it not*, to him it is sin" (James 4:17; italics added). This will be the case with those who simply believe. If indeed one does *believe*, why doesn't he *do* the things that God requires?

There is a huge difference between immortality and eternal

WHERE AM I GOING AFTER I DIE?

life. To be immortal means to live forever in a resurrected state, the tangible body and the spirit, or soul, having been reunited. Eternal life is the kind of life God and Jesus Christ live. Eternal life is reserved for those who are willing to pay the full price of obedience to the laws and commandments of God. Those who gain such an inheritance in the highest degree of heaven—the celestial kingdom—are those who are "joint-heirs" (see Romans 8:17) with Jesus Christ.

In the final judgment, each of us will be assigned to that degree of glory (kingdom) to which our beliefs, obedience, and works have qualified us. The doctrine of degrees of salvation should come as no surprise to anyone who reads and professes a belief in the Bible. In his second letter to the Corinthians, Paul states that he was "caught up to the *third heaven*" and "heard unspeakable words, which it is not lawful for a man to utter" (2 Corinthians 12:2, 4; italics added). Earlier, in his first letter, he spoke of the resurrection of the dead and he described "celestial bodies," "bodies terrestrial" (1 Corinthians 15:40), each pertaining to a different degree of glory. Then, speaking of the different glories, he said, "There is one glory of the sun, and another glory of the moon, and another glory of the stars: for one star differeth from another star in glory" (1 Corinthians 15:41). This truth was plainly taught in Paul's day. This is one more truth that has been restored to the earth today.

In his writings, Paul initially identified two of the degrees of glory, the first being the celestial and the second being the terrestrial. For some reason, probably through faulty translation, the third, the telestial, was omitted. However, the Lord restored a knowledge of the three degree of glory through the Prophet Joseph Smith.

Speaking of the qualifications for each kingdom the Lord

taught through Joseph, starting with the highest, the celestial, or the glory of the sun:

> They are they who received the testimony of Jesus, and believed on his name and were baptized after the manner of his burial, being buried in the water in his name, and this according to the commandment which he has given—
>
> That by keeping the commandments they might be washed and cleansed from all their sins, and receive the Holy Spirit by the laying on of the hands of him who is ordained and sealed unto this power;
>
> And who overcome by faith, and are sealed by the Holy Spirit of promise, which the Father sheds forth upon all those who are just and true.
>
> They are they who are the church of the Firstborn.
>
> They are they into whose hands the Father has given all things. (Doctrine and Covenants 76:51–55)

Then he spoke of the terrestrial, or the glory of the moon.

> Behold, these are they who died without law;
>
> And also they who are the spirits of men kept in prison, whom the Son visited, and preached the gospel unto them, that they might be judged according to men in the flesh;
>
> Who received not the testimony of Jesus in the flesh, but afterwards received it.
>
> These are they who are honorable men of the earth, who were blinded by the craftiness of men.
>
> These are they who receive of his glory, but not of his fulness.
>
> These are they who receive of the presence of the Son, but not of the fulness of the Father.

Wherefore, they are bodies terrestrial, and not bodies celestial, and differ in glory as the moon differs from the sun.

These are they who are not valiant in the testimony of Jesus; wherefore, they obtain not the crown over the kingdom of our God. (Doctrine and Covenants 76:72–79)

And next, he spoke of the telestial kingdom, or the glory of the stars.

These are they who received not the gospel of Christ, neither the testimony of Jesus.

These are they who deny not the Holy Spirit.

These are they who are thrust down to hell.

These are they who shall not be redeemed from the devil until the last resurrection, until the Lord, even Christ the Lamb, shall have finished his work.

These are they who receive not of his fulness in the eternal world, but of the Holy Spirit through the ministration of the terrestrial. (Doctrine and Covenants 76:82–86)

Then Joseph spoke of the last group, those who are "cast down to hell."

These are they who are liars, and sorcerers, and adulterers, and whoremongers, and whosoever loves and makes a lie.

These are they who suffer the wrath of God on earth.

These are they who suffer the vengeance of eternal fire.

These are they who are cast down to hell and suffer

the wrath of Almighty God, until the fulness of times, when Christ shall have subdued all enemies under his feet, and shall have perfected his work. (Doctrine and Covenants 76:103–106)

Considering that men will live their lives based upon their beliefs (whatever they may be), and considering that relatively few believe the same things or behave the same way, doesn't it stand to reason that a God of justice, love, and mercy would prepare for such a contingency? Therefore, each person is rewarded "according to his works" (Revelation 20:12) just as John the Revelator foresaw.

We've talked about salvation, now let's take a moment and discuss the true meaning of being damned. Many Christians are of the belief that being damned is being cast into hell for all eternity. For some, that will indeed be the case. But for the vast majority of those who chose not to live up to the fullness of the gospel law, those who failed to keep their second estates, those who will not be found worth by Christ to return back into the presence of Heavenly Father, they will be assigned a glory in either the terrestrial kingdom or the telestial kingdom. So how are such damned if they receive a glory? Those who attain eternal life, the kind of lives God and Christ live, will *progress* onward throughout the eternities.

Those in the lower kingdoms (terrestrial and telestial) are damned in that their progression has been stopped. Just like a dam stops the progression of a river, receiving a lesser glory damns, or stops, any further progression of those individuals whose lives warranted such a glory. God is just!

Salvation in any degree is determined by one thing—Christ declared, "He that believeth and is baptized shall be saved; but he that believeth not shall be damned" (Mark 16:16). And again,

"Verily, verily, I say unto thee, Except a man be born of water and of the Spirit, he cannot enter into the kingdom of God" (John 3:5). That's extraordinarily clear. So what becomes of all those men and women who have been born, lived, and died without ever hearing of Jesus Christ and never been baptized? According to the Lord himself, they are "damned," meaning they "cannot enter into the kingdom of God." Where is the justice in that?

Let's quote from the Book of Moses, in the Pearl of Great Price, one more time where God, speaking through Moses, said, "For behold, this is my work and my glory—to bring to pass the immortality and eternal life of man" (Moses 1:39). If this is indeed His work, then wouldn't it, for the most part, be greatly frustrated by the billions who have never heard of Christ, through no fault of their own, being cast out forever? Would a just God damn entire generations and whole nations simply because the Gospel was never available to them?

Anyone who lives and thinks with the Light of Christ should know that God, being no respecter of persons, loves all His children equally. This is another of those truths that is self-evident. In God's eyes, there is no difference between the living and the dead. They are all His children. He is mindful of them all wherever they may be in the course of progression.

During his mortal ministry, Jesus made a very interesting remark in these regards. He acknowledged, "The hour is coming, and now is, when the dead shall hear the voice of the Son of God: and they that hear shall live" (John 5:25). At the time, he was ministering to those who were alive. Soon he would die and minister to those in the spirit world, those who were dead. They would be given the opportunity to hear the Gospel, accept it or reject it, just as people did then and do today. Those who accept it would live and be, as it were, born again.

The Apostle Peter described the realization of Jesus's words in his first general Epistle:

> For it is better, if the will of God be so, that ye suffer for well doing, than for evil doing.
>
> "For Christ also hath once suffered for sins, the just for the unjust, that he might bring us to God, being put to death in the flesh, but quickened by the Spirit:
>
> By which also *he went and preached unto the spirits in prison*;
>
> Which sometime were disobedient, when once the longsuffering of God waited in the days of Noah (1 Peter 3:17–20; italics added).

Using some basic reasoning again, let me ask you: of what value would it be to preach the Gospel in the spirit world to the dead if the dead who believed couldn't repent and be saved? In the same epistle Peter makes it clear that all men "shall give account to him that is ready to judge the quick and the dead" (1 Peter 4:5). God loves all His children equally. He's not a respecter of persons. He is a just God, and "*for this cause was the gospel preached also to them that are dead*, that they might be judged according to men in the flesh, but live according to God in the spirit" (1 Peter 4:6; italics added). If those who had died without a knowledge of Christ couldn't have salvation offered to them as it had been offered to the living, then God would be neither just nor merciful. And if that were true, He would cease to be God.

They've heard the Gospel, some will have accepted it. Now, they must be baptized. But wait, how can the dead be baptized for the remission of sins not having bodies? Baptism is one of the saving ordinances, and no one can receive salvation without it (see John 3:5). It's an earthly ordinance. It's sound doctrine that those who are alive, and worthy, can be baptized, vicariously, for the dead. To do something vicariously for someone means to do for them that which they can't do for themselves. The atonement was a vicarious act by Jesus for all of us. Because of our fallen nature (being mortal and imperfect) we couldn't atone for our own sins. It was done in our behalf. We can accept the atonement, believe and obey and live accordingly, or we can reject it. If we reject it, it's as though it had never been done. The same is true with baptism for the dead. They can accept or reject it. If the dead individual accepts the baptism done for them (having heard and accepted the Gospel when it was preached to them), and they believe and obey and live accordingly within their sphere, then our act in their behalf is effective. If they reject it, it's as though it had never been done. It was in these regards that Paul made the statement, "Else what shall they do which are baptized for the dead, if the dead rise not at all? why are they then baptized for the dead?" (1 Corinthians 15:29). Paul was addressing those who, like the Sadducees, didn't believe in a resurrection. It's perfectly clear that at that time people were doing baptisms for their dead with a full understanding of the gospel doctrines pertaining to the resurrection and vicarious works for the dead.

So by all this, we can clearly see there was a need for a restitution of this doctrine. Also, we can see that these things have indeed been restored in these latter days. Isn't this evidence of an infinitely benevolent God? If these things are true, then God is merciful and just. If they aren't true, then God doesn't exercise justice and He hasn't the capacity for mercy.

Burden of Proof

*N*apoleon Hill, motivational speaker and author of the bestselling book *Think and Grow Rich*, acknowledged "No accurate thinker will judge another person by that which the other person's enemies say about him."

This book was written as the result of numerous falsehoods that are currently being perpetuated by those who are less than honest and truthful. This year (2007) alone we've had a member of the Church running for the Republican nomination for president of the United States. The recent broadcast of a lopsided, inaccurate documentary about Mormons broadcast on PBS, a weekly television program, about an obnoxious doctor with a supporting character who is a Mormon that is perpetuating misinformation about the Church, and on top of that, a group of evangelicals produced a video they claim was produced "out of love for our Lord Jesus Christ and love for our Mormon and Christian friends." Yet the video contains a thoroughly dishonest portrayal of the Mormon faith, using smear tactics and religious bigotry to perpetuate the same tired half-truths and misinformation that have been used for over 175 years. As a result of all this, the Church has been brought to the forefront of the news. And, if I may speak frankly, it is very tiresome reading and hearing and seeing what other people—nonmembers— outside the Church are claiming our doctrines to be. How ridiculous! The only thing more ridiculous is giving credence

Let's face it. The Gospel of Jesus Christ isn't a commodity. It's not a product you go online to do a Google search on to see what other users have had to say about the merchandise.

to such individuals and their falsehoods and half-truths.

Along similar lines, it was interesting to learn that a new study published in the October 30, 2007, issue of *Proceedings of the National Academy of Sciences* showed people are influenced by gossip to the point that they are willing to accept it as true even when their own observations and experiences suggest otherwise. What a sad statement!

Among those who persecute the Church, there are former members who have become disaffected for whatever reason. Experience has taught, you can leave the Church, but you can't leave it alone. Why is that? The answer is simple: Once the Holy Ghost has given an individual a witness of the truth and divinity of this work, once he has accepted it, that person steps over the line from Satan's side to the Lord's side. There is only one way for someone to lose his testimony, and that's by giving in to the temptations of the devil. Satan isn't content with the individual simply leaving the Church, he directs that individual to come out in open rebellion against the Church and all it teaches. Many of these people have attempted to warn others—through books, Web sites, and videos—about the wicked Mormon church. Based on their description of the church they belonged to and based on the facts of the Church I belong to, they are two entirely different churches.

Let's face it. The Gospel of Jesus Christ isn't a commodity. It's not a product you go online to do a Google search on to see what other users have had to say about the merchandise. That's not how a testimony of truth is gained.

Time and time again, as history has shown, the enemies of the Church constantly use a technique of argument known as a straw man. That is, they attribute a teaching to the Church that the Church doesn't teach. Such individuals know they can't fight truth fairly and successfully, so they attribute false doctrines to the Church, thus creating a straw man they can then begin to beat the life out of as if it had any life to begin with.

This straw man concept is the principal tool in the anti-Mormon's tool chest. The usual method to prop up the straw man is to quote a Mormon leader as having made some comment related to their straw man issue. However, and this is most important, don't ever quote a leader who is still alive. The longer he's been dead, the better! Then they demand proof to refute what they've presented.

While working on this book, I received an e-mail from someone, who isn't a member of the Church, demanding that I provide proof that the Book of Mormon is true. I didn't even attempt to provide any such proof. Why? The burden of proof wasn't mine. Consider this: if I were in debt to you for one hundred dollars and I attempted to pay that debt with a crisp, brand-new one hundred dollar bill and you wouldn't take it, claiming it was counterfeit, the burden of proof would be yours, not mine. That's the rule of law.

Who can disprove that Moses spoke with God face-to-face? Who can disprove that Joshua commanded the sun and the moon to stand still? Who can disprove that Jesus was the Christ? Who can disprove that Lazarus was raised from the dead? Who can disprove that Christ was resurrected? Who can disprove that the Lord appeared, after his resurrection, to Mary Magdalene in the garden and the apostles in the upper room?

In more than two thousand years, has anyone been able to disprove anything relating to biblical claims? The chief apostle, Peter, testified, speaking not only for himself but also for the other apostles as well:

> And we are witnesses of all things which he did both in the land of the Jews, and in Jerusalem; whom they slew and hanged on a tree:
>
> Him God raised up the third day, and shewed him openly;
>
> Not to all the people, but unto witnesses chosen before of God, even to us, who did eat and drink with him after he rose from the dead.
>
> And he commanded us to preach unto the people, and to testify that it is he which was ordained of God to be the Judge of quick and dead (Acts 10:39–42).

Who, after all these centuries, has disproved Peter's witness?

So I ask you, what's the difference between Peter's testimony and the one given by Joseph Smith and Sidney Rigdon when they declared,

> And now, after the many testimonies which have been given of him, this is the testimony, last of all, which we give of him: That he lives!
>
> For we saw him, even on the right hand of God; and we heard the voice bearing record that he is the Only Begotten of the Father—
>
> That by him, and through him, and of him, the worlds are and were created, and the inhabitants thereof are begotten sons and daughters unto God (Doctrine and Covenants 76:22–24)?

What evidence can be given to prove that a prophet hasn't

had such experiences? Speaking of his first experience, when the Father and the Son appeared to him in the grove, the young Prophet Joseph testified, "I have actually seen a vision; and who am I that I can withstand God, or why does the world think to make me deny what I have actually seen? For I had seen a vision; I knew it, and I knew that God knew it, and I could not deny it, neither dared I do it; at least I knew that by so doing I would offend God, and come under condemnation" (JSH 1:25).

Either we accept the testimonies of the prophets or we reject them. There is no debate. There is no need for hostility. Jesus Christ neither debated nor argued with the Sadducees and the Pharisees. He answered their questions and that was the end of it. They either accepted his answers or they rejected them. These two groups were continuously hounding Jesus for proof of his divinity. Yet when it was given, time after time, they *chose* to ignore it. It wasn't because the evidence wasn't provided, it was because they didn't want to believe. When those who attack truth stand and demand proof, that's the last thing they want. Those who claim that The Church of Jesus Christ of Latter-day Saints is false bear the burden of proof as did those who railed against the prophets, apostles, and Christ himself anciently.

Those who seek proof are really no different than those who seek after a sign. What did the Lord say about those who seek after a sign (proof)? "An evil and adulterous generation seeketh after a sign" (Matthew 12:39). Hadn't Christ given plenty of signs? How many signs are required? How many signs are enough? Is it one? Is it ten? Is it a hundred? Is it a thousand? How many signs does the unbelieving heart require before it will believe? Such seekers aren't satisfied with the truth.

A preacher once approached Joseph Smith demanding a

sign. The man's name was Hayden. He said that he had come a considerable distance to be convinced of the truth.

"Why," said he, "Mr. Smith, I want to know the truth, and when I am convinced, I will spend all my talents and time in defending and spreading the doctrines of your religion, and I will give you to understand that to convince me is equivalent to convincing all my society, amounting to several hundreds."

Joseph started telling the man about the coming forth of the Book of Mormon, the first principles of the Gospel, and so on, then Hayden exclaimed, "O this is not the evidence I want, the evidence that I wish to have is a notable miracle; I want to see some powerful manifestation of the power of God, I want to see a notable miracle performed; and if you perform such a one, then I will believe with all my heart and soul, and will exert all my power and all my extensive influence to convince others; and if you will not perform a miracle of this kind, then I am your worst and bitterest enemy."

"Well," said Joseph, "what will you have done? Will you be struck blind, or dumb? Will you be paralyzed, or will you have one hand withered? Take your choice, choose which you please, and in the name of the Lord Jesus Christ it shall be done."

"That is not the kind of miracle I want," said the preacher.

"Then, sir," replied Joseph, "I can perform none. I am not going to bring any trouble upon any body else, sir, to convince you. I will tell you what you make me think of— the very first person who asked a sign of the Savior, for it is written, in the New Testament, that Satan came to the Savior in the desert, when he was hungry with forty days' fasting, and said, 'If you be the Son of God, command these stones to be made bread.'

"And now," said Joseph, "the children of the devil and his servants have been asking for signs ever since; and when the

The Lord has made it abundantly clear that faith doesn't come by signs or miracles.

people in that day continued asking him for signs to prove the truth of the gospel which he preached, the Savior replied, 'It is a wicked and an adulterous generation that seeketh a sign'" (*Journal of Discourses*, 2:326–27).

God doesn't provide signs or miracles to satisfy curiosity. Signs and miracles do not build faith. "Though he [Jesus] had done so many miracles before them, yet they believed not on him" (John 12:37). The Lord has made it abundantly clear that faith doesn't come by signs or miracles.

Those who are honestly seeking to know if the Book of Mormon is true or not don't seek after signs. However, they are required to understand and apply the following five principles:

1. Desire
2. Humility
3. Study
4. Prayer
5. Practice

Desire – In the quest for spiritual truth, one must first have a genuine desire for truth. That desire must be a driving force. Anything less simply won't do. Without that driving force— that burning—the individual will not be willing to pay the price required for a testimony of the truth. And there is a price to be paid!

Humility – Those who desire truth must be willing to recognize their own limitations. The honest seeker of truth, he who is humble, will recognize the necessity of means far beyond his own mortal comprehension in order to gain spiritual truth (see 1 Corinthians 2:9–16). The student must admit there is One who is the Divine Source to all truth. Only with the aid of God can the student ever hope to gain a knowledge of the truth. The two must work together, with the student taking the subservient position.

Study – There must be an honest effort on the part of the student to read the Book of Mormon (all scripture for that matter) and try his best to understand (ponder) what's being said. Once he has expended all his understanding (and in most cases that doesn't take us long), then he can pray to God for further light and knowledge on the subject at hand.

Prayer – The student asks if what he is reading is true. He asks, is it of man or is it of God? The student must pray for knowledge and answers and it has to be done with real intent and an honest heart. These prayers must be as insistent and constant as the desire itself. The prayers must be offered in the name of Jesus Christ, having faith that they will be answered in God's own time, not ours.

Practice – The principles that are taught in the scriptures must be applied; they must be practiced. "Be ye doers of the word, and not hearers only, deceiving your own selves" (James 1:22). Part of learning the truth of the Gospel is applying its teachings. You may read what others say, you may see what others do, but the time comes when each of us must find out for ourselves, and that will only happen when we become "doers" ourselves.

Those who attempt to pass judgment on the restored Gospel of Jesus Christ, or the Book of Mormon, without following these God-given steps are not seeking after truth, and their opinions of them are totally worthless.

Jesus invited all of us to test the truths given him by his Father:

"My doctrine is not mine, but his that sent me.

"If any man *will do his will*, he shall know of the doctrine, whether it be of God, or whether I speak of myself" (John 7:16–17; italics added).

And again,

"If I do not the works of my Father, believe me not.

"But if I do, though ye believe not me, believe the works: that ye may know, and believe, that the Father is in me, and I in him" (John 10:37–38).

Once more,

"Let your light so shine before men, *that they may see your good works*, and glorify your Father which is in heaven" (Matthew 5:16; italics added).

The person of whom I spoke earlier who demanded proof, I asked, "Are you seeking after truth, or are you seeking to disprove?" There is a big difference between the two. I explained that seeking truth (testing) must be sincere and honest. The restored Gospel's truth or goodness must be what is being sought, not some untruth or evil. Any untruth or evil that exists, if it's there, will be found automatically.

Early on in the course of our electronic discussion he said something to the effect that God gave us a mind to reason with. I agreed and offered the challenge that is found toward the end of the Book of Mormon. They are the closing words of the prophet Moroni (the same who visited Joseph Smith) in the last chapter of the last book in that volume of scripture.

> Behold, I would exhort you that when ye shall read these things, if it be wisdom in God that ye should read them, that ye would remember how merciful the Lord hath been unto the children of men, from the creation of Adam even down until the time that ye shall receive these things, and ponder it in your hearts.

> And when ye shall receive these things, I would
> exhort you that ye would ask God, the Eternal Father,
> in the name of Christ, if these things are not true; and
> if ye shall ask with a sincere heart, with real intent,
> having faith in Christ, he will manifest the truth of it
> unto you, by the power of the Holy Ghost.
>
> And by the power of the Holy Ghost ye may
> know the truth of all things. (Moroni 10:3–5)

I told the doubter, either the above quote is totally true or it is totally false. Which is it? Let's test it and see. Let's apply some reasoning by asking some qualifying questions:

The Lord is merciful to the children of men. True or False. *Exodus 34:6; Luke 6:36*

The scriptures urge men to pray to God for answers. True or False. *James 1:5*

When men approach God, they must be sincere—truthful. True or False. *Matthew 21:22*

When men approach God in prayer, they must have real intent—an honest desire. True or False. *Mark 11:24*

It is necessary that men exercise faith—belief in Jesus Christ. True or False. *John 11:26; 14:6*

God can manifest the truth of all things. True or False. *1 Corinthians 2:10*

The Holy Ghost does teach all truth. True or False. *1 Corinthians 2:13*

Throughout the course of our conversation, he ignored these true/false statements. When pressed on giving answers, he acknowledged the answers to all were true. So my question to him, and anyone else who may read that exhortation, was why are you unwilling to apply it? He never answered.

There are four basic questions one must honestly answer

if he claims to be seeking truth as it pertains to the Book of Mormon.

1. Am I looking for truth, or am I looking to disprove something?

2. Am I willing to sit down and read the Book of Mormon?

3. Am I willing to apply the steps as given to find the truth?

4. Am I willing to accept the truth when it's revealed and act upon it?

Unfortunately, that last one seems to be the sticking point for most people.

Why do those who profess a belief in the Bible attack the Book of Mormon, claiming that its teachings are false and even of the devil? The irony is the vast majority of its opponents have never read a single verse. Contained in the Book of Mormon is another passage written by Moroni. Read it. Weigh its words, based on the knowledge you have today. Reason it out in your mind and see if what it says is true.

> For behold…it is given unto you to judge, that ye may know good from evil; and the way to judge is as plain, that ye may know with a perfect knowledge, as the daylight is from the dark night.
>
> For behold, the Spirit of Christ is given to every man, that he may know good from evil; wherefore, I show unto you the way to judge; for every thing which inviteth to do good, and to persuade to believe in Christ, is sent forth by the power and gift of Christ; wherefore ye may know with a perfect knowledge it is of God.
>
> But whatsoever thing persuadeth men to do evil,

and believe not in Christ, and deny him, and serve not God, then ye may know with a perfect knowledge it is of the devil; for after this manner doth the devil work, for he persuadeth no man to do good, no, not one; neither do his angels; neither do they who subject themselves unto him. (Moroni 7:15–17)

So what do you think? Is that declaration true or is it false? Do those sound like the words of Christ, or do those sound like the words of an evil, designing man? Once more, let's reason this out and discover the answer for ourselves.

Does God desire that we know good from evil? Yes or no?

Is the Spirit (Light) of Christ given to everyone? Yes or no?

Is it by this Spirit that we can know good from evil? Yes or no?

Does Christ invite us to do good? Yes or no?

Does Christ want us to believe (have faith) in him? Yes or no?

Does all that is good come from God? Yes or no?

Does that which persuades us to do evil come from the devil? Yes or no?

Does the devil persuade us to deny Christ? Yes or no?

Does the devil persuade men to do anything that is good? Yes or no?

Okay, what, then, is the answer as to the truthfulness of that passage given by Moroni? All that he said is accurate, isn't it? Of course it is.

That being the case, let's consider some of the themes and doctrines taught in this book (the Book of Mormon) that so many claim to be of the devil.

- Jesus is the Christ
- Jesus Christ atoned for the sins of mankind

- No man can be saved except through Jesus Christ
- Obedience to God's commandments
- It requires faith to follow God's commandments
- Jews will be gathered and restored to their rightful place
- Men are saved by God's good grace
- The kingdom of God will triumph
- Those who are righteous are favored of God
- The righteous need not fear
- God will not forget His covenants or His covenant people
- The words of the prophet Isaiah are true
- Prior to the Second Coming God would restore all things
- The need for baptism and the gift of the Holy Ghost
- Keeping one's heart upon the things of God
- Our indebtedness to God
- Becoming sons and daughters of Christ
- Being in harmony with God
- Being faithful to God even until death
- Repent of sins and turn to Christ
- Entering the rest of the Lord
- Bring souls unto Christ through love
- Wickedness never was happiness
- Freedom and liberty are worth fighting for
- Little children are sinless and innocent before God
- Listen to God's prophets
- Men need to prepare for the Second Coming
- Principles that lead to sanctification
- Christ visits his "other sheep"
- Remember Christ's atonement
- Search the scriptures
- Prophecies of the latter days prior to the Second Coming

- Faith is tried through trials and tribulation
- The way to Christ
- Becoming perfect in Christ

Granted, these are broad general themes, but what among them is so objectionable that anyone should be killed for preaching them? What is listed here that warrants so much animosity and persecution from others who profess to be Christian and who profess to be followers of Jesus Christ?

The Book of Mormon shows us how to discern good from evil. It invites men and women everywhere to come unto Christ. It teaches how to exercise faith in Jesus Christ. It teaches that all things that are good come from God for the benefit of mankind. It teaches of Jesus Christ as said by Nephi, one of the prophet writers.

> We labor diligently to write, to persuade our children, and also our brethren, to believe in Christ, and to be reconciled to God; for we know that it is by grace that we are saved, after all we can do.
>
> And, notwithstanding we believe in Christ…and look forward with steadfastness unto Christ, until the law shall be fulfilled.
>
> …and we are made alive in Christ because of our faith…
>
> And we talk of Christ, we rejoice in Christ, we preach of Christ, we prophesy of Christ, and we write according to our prophecies, that our children may know to what source they may look for a remission of their sins. (2 Nephi 25:23–26)

Now, I ask you, please, tell me if you can, what's wrong with that passage? Based on the standard given by Moroni on determining good from evil, where is the evil in those words? What is contained in those words that would cause one Christian to attack and demean another?

"Well, you've only provided a few passages. What else does the Book of Mormon have to say? It's hard to decide, based on these few verses." You're right. Since I obviously can't print the entire book here, go to Appendix B and there you'll find information on how to get your own copy at no cost.

Speaking of the Book of Mormon specifically, the fundamental question it asks is, "Do you want to learn more of Christ?" The purpose of the Book of Mormon, as stated on its title page, is "to the convincing of the Jew and Gentile that Jesus is the Christ, the Eternal God." How is that blasphemous?

The Book of Mormon prophet Nephi declared, "For the fulness of mine intent is that I may persuade men to come unto the God of Abraham, and the God of Isaac, and the God of Jacob, and be saved.

"Wherefore, the things which are pleasing unto the world I do not write, but the things which are pleasing unto God and unto those who are not of the world" (1 Nephi 6:4–5).

I've already mentioned the Book of Mormon is, first of all, another testament of Jesus Christ and shows us how to draw nearer to him. Second, the Book of Mormon confounds false doctrines and exposes the enemies of God. It was written for us in our day under the inspiration of God with His infinite foreknowledge. The problems and challenges of the peoples in the Book of Mormon times are reflected in the problems and challenges we face today as they pertain to false religious, political, philosophical, and educational ideologies.

Referring to the Book of Mormon, the Prophet Joseph Smith said that the book was "the keystone of our religion" (*History of the Church*, vol. 4, p. 461). A keystone is the architectural piece at the crown of an arch which locks the other stones into position, upholding the arch. Remove the keystone and the arch collapses. The Book of Mormon is true or it is false. If it is false, then The Church of Jesus Christ of Latter-day Saints collapses. Yet, after one hundred seventy-seven years of attack, the Book of Mormon and the Church stand stronger than ever.

Regardless of what specific doctrine or doctrines of the Church a dissenter may object to, the only real problem that dissenter has to resolve is whether or not the Book of Mormon is true. If the book is true, then Jesus is the Christ. If the Book of Mormon is true, then Joseph Smith was his prophet. If the Book of Mormon is true, then The Church of Jesus Christ of Latter-day Saints and its doctrines are true. If the Book of Mormon is true, then a prophet leads the Church today by receiving revelation from God.

Now, I understand that not everyone will accept these things. I respect that. However, why do those who disbelieve, those who call themselves Christians, fight so vehemently against those of us who are members of the Church and ridicule so harshly that which is sacred?

By Their Fruits

*I*n the previous chapter I had mentioned that a member of the Church was running for the Republican nomination for president. Just last week I was reading a news article about that candidate and the issue of "Mormons as Christians," which keeps cropping up time and time again, especially among evangelical Christians. A recent survey showed that many of these evangelicals are drawn to this candidate's values but repelled by his Mormon faith. Can you see the inconsistency in that statement? Isn't that like saying, "I like apples, but I am repulsed by apple trees"? How can one accept the teachings of Jesus Christ but reject the Savior?

More times than I care to count, I've read or heard how people really admire Mormons for their family values, yet their teachings are abhorrent. Mormons are held in high regard because of their work ethic, but the Prophet Joseph Smith was a scoundrel. Mormons are respected for their moral points of view on chastity, honesty, abstinence from alcohol, tobacco, and drugs, yet their doctrines are of the devil. Mormons are appreciated for their humanitarian contributions and the goods and services provided in the wake of natural catastrophes around the world; nevertheless, they aren't considered Christians. Where has there ever been a greater contradiction of thought? Where do people think our values and morals come from?

WHAT'S WRONG WITH MORMONS?

Who do these detractors presume the Source of these values and morals to be?

Our Savior, Jesus Christ, asked, "Do men gather grapes of thorns, or figs of thistles?" He went on to explain, "Even so every good tree bringeth forth good fruit; but a corrupt tree bringeth forth evil fruit. A good tree cannot bring forth evil fruit, neither can a corrupt tree bring forth good fruit" (Matthew 7:16–18). It is a rank impossibility for anything that is good to come from anything that is evil. In these regards, either something is all good or it is all bad. Pure water cannot be drawn from a polluted well. Many Mormons are seen as the pillars of their communities, but are believed to follow blasphemies and lies. Speaking of those that follow his teachings and live his doctrines, the Lord said, "Wherefore by their fruits ye shall know them" (Matthew 7:20). The good fruits of this Church are seen and known around the world. Yet there are those who would chop down the tree from which those fruits come and cast it into the fire. Such thinking flies in the face of logic.

If the fruits of the tree of the restored Gospel are sweet, then how can it be that its roots are rotten? Christ himself gave us the standard by which we might know the truth. He said, "My doctrine is not mine, but his that sent me. If any man will do his will, he shall know of the doctrine, whether it be of God, or whether I speak of myself" (John 7:16–17). Is there any one person who can't do that if he is willing and truly seeking after Christ? We can apply the restored doctrine in our lives and by doing so we can experience the Christlike spirit growing within us. The only way to learn the truth—experience the fruits—is to put it to the test. So early on I decided I would. What an eye-opener!

One of the first worship services I attended with Linda and her family was what's referred to as fast and testimony meeting.

This meeting is held on the first Sunday of each month (in place of the regular sacrament meeting). The members are admonished to fast, to go without food and drink for two consecutive meals, and give at least the amount of money saved from those two meals (referred to as a fast offering) to the bishop in order to help the poor in that ward (congregation).

The beginning of this meeting was similar to any other I had attended in various churches. There was an opening hymn, the invocation, some brief announcements, and ward business. Then there was another hymn in preparation for the sacrament (communion), which was passed to the members. Once that was completed, the remainder of the meeting was given to the members to stand and bear their testimonies.

I don't remember exactly who it was (it was probably the bishop who had been conducting the meeting), but he said something like, "Brothers and sisters, I want to take this opportunity to share with you my testimony of the restored Gospel of Jesus Christ. I know this is the only true Church on the face of the earth today…"

Wait a minute! Excuse me…? I thought as I bowed up in the back. What I had just heard was a bite of bitter fruit, almost too bitter to swallow. My first reaction was one of indignation and anger. *How dare you say such a thing!* What followed was what felt like an endless procession of various members going up to the pulpit and sharing like testimonies, each referring to The Church of Jesus Christ of Latter-day Saints as the "only true Church." I wondered where they got off saying such a thing.

However, as I sat there and listened to those individuals speak from their hearts, I noticed mine began to soften. Some of them spoke of the divinity of Joseph Smith's calling as a prophet. Others spoke of the truthfulness of the Book of Mormon and its teachings. Still others spoke of what a blessing it is to have a prophet on the earth today. As I sat there weighing these things in my mind, the anger and indignation began to fade. Although I didn't fully understand everything I had heard—not even a fraction of it—by the end of that meeting I felt at peace with these people, just like I had with Linda and her family.

During one of my Sunday evening conversations with the missionaries, early on they pointed out a passage in the Book of Mormon in which the prophet Alma discusses faith and the word (meaning the Word of God) and testing the fruits of it. In this passage he uses the metaphor of planting a seed.

> Now, as I said concerning faith—that it was not a perfect knowledge—even so it is with my words. Ye cannot know of their surety at first, unto perfection, any more than faith is a perfect knowledge.
>
> But behold, if ye will awake and arouse your faculties, even to an experiment upon my words, and exercise a particle of faith, yea, even if ye can no more than desire to believe, let this desire work in you, even until ye believe in a manner that ye can give place for a portion of my words.
>
> Now, we will compare the word unto a seed. Now, if ye give place, that a seed may be planted in your heart, behold, if it be a true seed, or a good seed, if ye do not cast it out by your unbelief, that ye will resist the Spirit of the Lord, behold, it will begin to swell within your breasts; and when you feel these swelling motions, ye will begin to say within yourselves—It must needs be that this is a good seed, or that the word is good, for it beginneth to enlarge my soul; yea, it beginneth to enlighten my understanding, yea, it beginneth to be delicious to me.

Now behold, would not this increase your faith? I say unto you, Yea; nevertheless it hath not grown up to a perfect knowledge.

But behold, as the seed swelleth, and sprouteth, and beginneth to grow, then you must needs say that the seed is good; for behold it swelleth, and sprouteth, and beginneth to grow. And now, behold, will not this strengthen your faith? Yea, it will strengthen your faith: for ye will say I know that this is a good seed; for behold it sprouteth and beginneth to grow.

And now, behold, are ye sure that this is a good seed? I say unto you, Yea; for every seed bringeth forth unto its own likeness.

Therefore, if a seed groweth it is good, but if it groweth not, behold it is not good, therefore it is cast away.

And now, behold, because ye have tried the experiment, and planted the seed, and it swelleth and sprouteth, and beginneth to grow, ye must needs know that the seed is good.

And now, behold, is your knowledge perfect? Yea, your knowledge is perfect in that thing, and your faith is dormant; and this because you know, for ye know that the word hath swelled your souls, and ye also know that it hath sprouted up, that your understanding doth begin to be enlightened, and your mind doth begin to expand.

O then, is not this real? I say unto you, Yea, because it is light; and whatsoever is light, is good, because it is discernible, therefore ye must know that it is good; and now behold, after ye have tasted this light is your knowledge perfect?

Behold I say unto you, Nay; neither must ye lay aside your faith, for ye have only exercised your faith to plant the seed that ye might try the experiment to know if the seed was good.

And behold, as the tree beginneth to grow, ye will say: Let us nourish it with great care, that it may get root, that it may grow up, and bring forth fruit unto us. And now behold, if ye nourish it with much care it will get root, and grow up, and bring forth fruit.

But if ye neglect the tree, and take no thought for its nourishment, behold it will not get any root; and when the heat of the sun cometh and scorcheth it, because it hath no root it withers away, and ye pluck it up and cast it out.

Now, this is not because the seed was not good, neither is it because the fruit thereof would not be desirable; but it is because your ground is barren, and ye will not nourish the tree, therefore ye cannot have the fruit thereof.

And thus, if ye will not nourish the word, looking forward with an eye of faith to the fruit thereof, ye can never pluck of the fruit of the tree of life.

But if ye will nourish the word, yea, nourish the tree as it beginneth to grow, by your faith with great diligence, and with patience, looking forward to the fruit thereof, it shall take root; and behold it shall be a tree springing up unto everlasting life.

And because of your diligence and your faith and your patience with the word in nourishing it, that it may take root in you, behold, by and by ye shall pluck the fruit thereof, which is most precious, which is sweet above all that is sweet, and which is white above all that is white, yea, and pure above all that is pure; and ye shall feast upon this fruit even until ye are filled, that ye hunger not, neither shall ye thirst.

Then, my brethren, ye shall reap the rewards of your faith, and your diligence, and patience, and long-suffering, waiting for the tree to bring forth fruit unto you. (Alma 32:26–43)

What a beautiful metaphor! Over thirty-two years ago I chose to "experiment" upon the word. I found Alma's words to be true, the fruit to be sweet.

Throughout the six-week discussion with the Mormon missionaries, I was encouraged to read the Book of Mormon and while doing so ask myself, "Could Joseph Smith have written this?" I was encouraged to pray and ask God if the Book of Mormon were true. So I did. I didn't have any pre-conceived ideas, no opinion of the truthfulness of the Book of Mormon, one way or the other. The only truth I knew was that I didn't know. I did believe that God answered prayers. I did believe that Jesus was the Christ who atoned for our sins. I did believe that by the Holy Ghost we could know the truth of whatever we might ask. So I asked, several times throughout our discussions, "Is this work of Thy hands, or is this the work of Joseph Smith?" And the answer I received each time was... nothing, nada, zilch, zip, zero. What I was hearing from the Elders felt good. My heart was at peace, my thoughts were calm and reflective, but I wasn't receiving any answers as to the truthfulness of the Book of Mormon.

It was late Saturday night. In less than twenty-four hours I would be having my last formal discussion with the missionaries. I sat in the same director's chair that I had sat in six weeks earlier wanting to die, reading several chapters, and preparing myself to ask Heavenly Father one last time if the Book of Mormon were true. As odd as it may sound, one of the things that sticks out most in my mind about that night was the throw rug I knelt on next to my bed. It was one of those old-fashioned braided oval rugs in varying shades of brown, rust, green, gold, and tan. I can still see it in my mind as if it were happening all over again. I knelt down with the Book of Mormon in hand and rested on the edge of the bed. I bowed my head, closed my eyes, and praying vocally, I asked Him one more time if the Book of Mormon were true. I pleaded with God to tell me, one way or the other, if it were true or if it was the work of Joseph Smith's imagination. I explained to Him that I was having my last discussion with the missionaries the next night, that I had tried very hard to do everything they had asked of me. I had put Alma's analogy of the seed to the test, and I told Him I would really appreciate an answer. Then, just as I was about to finish my prayer, I was bathed in a warm, peaceful feeling that words cannot describe. I heard the words in my mind, not in my own voice, "Yes, these things you have read are of me. The Book of Mormon is my word, which has been translated by the hand of my servant, Joseph Smith Jr. The things the missionaries have taught you are true. These things are not of men. They are of me." I was stunned to say the least.

There is really nothing more for me to say in these regards. What I can do is paraphrase Joseph Smith's words and say, "How can I contradict God? Why would anyone want me to deny what I've actually experienced? God gave me an answer; I knew it, and I knew that He knew it. I can't and won't deny it. By doing so I would offend God and come under condemnation."

Since that first spiritual experience, I have had (and continue to have) countless similar experiences in which the Holy

Ghost has whispered to me the truthfulness of many things, both church- and Gospel-related and things that were neither church- nor Gospel-related. I have had God reveal to me many things, some of which I wasn't actively seeking—much of it associated with my family and work. I cannot nor will I ever deny His power.

That next Sunday morning, I went to church early waiting for Linda, her family, and the missionaries. With a big smile on my face, I told them what had happened the night before.

Now, I know what those people who stood and bore their testimonies in that first fast and testimony meeting knew. Also, I understand all too well how those words "the only true Church" sound to nonmembers. They sting, painfully so. It's not unlike getting a shot from the doctor. There are times we have to endure some discomfort in order to regain our health.

The next evening, Monday, after I had gotten home from work and had my dinner, I got a phone call from the missionaries. They asked if I could come over to their apartment, that they had something to ask me. I jumped in the car and drove over to their place. Once there, they invited me inside and insisted that I sit in the only comfortable chair in the room. The senior of the two asked me if I would mind him asking me some questions. "Sure, go ahead," I answered.

He looked me straight in the eye and asked, "Do you believe in God the Eternal Father?"

"Yes!" I replied.

"Do you believe Jesus is the Christ?"

"Of course."

"Do you have a testimony of Joseph Smith as a prophet?"

"Yes, I do."

"Do you believe there is a prophet that leads the Lord's Church today?"

"Yes."

"Do you believe that the Book of Mormon is the Word of God?"

"Yes!" I was wondering where all this was leading. Then, after another couple of questions he asked, "Well then, are you willing to be baptized into the Church?"

I was a little surprised. I shot back, "Wait a minute. I never said anything about joining your Church."

He said, "No, you didn't. But you made it plain that you have been looking for the truth. Now that you've found it, don't you think you have an obligation to act upon it?"

I thought for a moment. I hadn't looked at it from that perspective. Then I remembered my mom and dad. What would they say about their youngest son joining the Mormons? Mom would probably kill me if she were close enough. Thank goodness I was in Raleigh, North Carolina, and she was in Nitro, West Virginia! Thoughts were flying around in my head at a hundred miles an hour. I weighed the possibilities, took a deep breath, and let it out saying, "I'm sorry, I can't do that. You don't understand, it would break my parents' hearts, especially my mom's."

Without missing a beat, the other Elder said, "Here, Brother Gladwell, read this," and he handed me his Bible. It was opened to Matthew chapter 10. "Read verses thirty-seven and thirty-eight out loud," he said.

"He that loveth father or mother more than me is not worthy of me: and he that loveth son or daughter more than me is not worthy of me.

"And he that taketh not his cross, and followeth after me, is not worthy of me."

Those words pierced my heart. It was as though the Lord were standing there speaking directly to me. I love my Savior

Telling my parents I was joining The Church of Jesus Christ of Latter-day Saints was the one of the most difficult things I've ever done.

more than anything. Was I going to pay lip service only or was I going to follow him? More than anything I wanted to be worthy of him. After all I had said and done over the past six weeks, after having received an answer to my prayer, after just bearing my testimony to the truthfulness of these things, how could I *not* follow him?

Telling my parents I was joining The Church of Jesus Christ of Latter-day Saints was the one of the most difficult things I've ever done. I tried to explain why, but they wouldn't listen. They weren't interested. You would have thought I had just told them I had been arrested for child molestation and drug dealing. Mom was especially angry and bitter, and I'm sure she was hurt too.

A week later, on Saturday, January 25, 1975, I was baptized by Linda's dad, Bill. Afterward, he laid his hands upon my head, along with the two missionaries, and by the power and authority of the Melchizedek priesthood, they confirmed me a member of the Church and gave me the gift of the Holy Ghost. Again, there are simply no words, in this or any language, that can describe how wonderful and clean I felt at that moment!

Do you remember the map that Linda's mom, Marie, gave me? She had drawn a circle around Raleigh and written *HOME* above it. Not only had Linda and her family shown me how to find my way back to Raleigh, should I ever get lost again, but also, more importantly, they showed me how to find my way back to my Heavenly Father and my heavenly home. In addition to all that, they also introduced me to Churé, my wife and eternal companion.

Since my first meeting with those Mormon elders, I have attempted to live Paul's admonition to "prove all things; hold fast that which is good" (1 Thessalonians 5:21). And over the years, and with the advent of grandchildren, my parents' hearts were softened. They learned through having a son, a daughter-in-law, and four grandchildren that are members of The Church of Jesus Christ of Latter-day Saints that Mormons are not bad. They learned that Mormons are just as much Christians as anyone. Although they had learned the truth about Mormons and understood and agreed with many of the doctrines, they never could find it within themselves to join the Church.

Dad died in 1995. Mom died in 2004. During our last telephone conversation, Mom and I knew it would probably be the last time we'd talk to one another. Toward the end of our chat she said, "Well, I guess I'm going to find out."

"Find out what?" I asked.

"Whether or not the Mormon church is true," she replied.

I told her, "There are easier ways to get the answer to that question."

As I said, by the time my parents died there was no animosity, there was no anger, there was no hatred, there was no rancor. They learned that the Church is not an evil organization. They learned that the doctrines of the restored Gospel were not blasphemous lies. They did learn, firsthand, that the falsehoods and the half-truths perpetuated by those who persecute the Church are exactly that.

It's not easy to be a member of The Church of Jesus Christ of Latter-day Saints. The Lord declared, "For unto whomsoever much is given, of him shall be much required" (Luke 12:48).

To come unto Christ, we must walk away from the world.

The Lord extended an invitation to everyone saying, "Come unto me" (Matthew 11:28). To come unto Christ, we must walk away from the world. To forsake the world is to forsake Satan and his influences. And when we step over that line from his side to the Lord's side, we become fair game for those who would persecute and scorn the followers of Christ. Consider the following statements of the Lord as he warned those who would take upon them his name:

"Blessed are ye, when men shall revile you, and persecute you, and shall say all manner of evil against you falsely, for my sake" (Matthew 5:11).

"And ye shall be hated of all men for my name's sake" (Matthew 10:22).

"Then shall they deliver you up to be afflicted, and shall kill you: and ye shall be hated of all nations for my name's sake" (Matthew 24:9).

These passages are the answer to the question I posed at the end of the previous chapter. Such is the fate of those who have truly taken upon themselves the name of Jesus Christ and follow in his footsteps.

For those of us who are members of The Church of Jesus Christ of Latter-day Saints we are so because the Holy Ghost has born an undeniable witness to us of the truthfulness of it. We have tested the word. We have tasted the fruits and found them to be good and desirable. We have taken God at His word when He said, "Prove me now herewith," and found Him to be true and He has opened the windows of heaven and poured out a blessing upon us (Malachi 3:10). As a result of this, we are willing to commit ourselves to worshipping God the Eternal

Father, to obeying the teachings of His Son, the Lord Jesus Christ, and to following the promptings of the Holy Ghost. We are committed to being morally clean; we refrain from using obscene and profane language; we strive to keep the Sabbath day holy; we pledge to be honest in all our dealings with our fellow man; we abstain from using illegal drugs, alcohol, and tobacco. We covenant to give of our own time, talents, and income in the service of others and to the building up of God's kingdom on earth. When we marry, we do so with a covenant to God to remain true and faithful to our spouse, not only for time, but also for eternity. As parents we do our best to rear children who not only honor their parents, but also honor their God and their Redeemer. We teach them to repent of their sins and turn to Christ for salvation. We encourage them to contribute to their community and to honor and obey the laws of the land. We covenant to be honest, true, chaste, benevolent, virtuous, and in doing good to all men. We seek after things that are virtuous, lovely, or of good report or praiseworthy.

So with the evidence of all these good fruits, having chosen to freely take upon us these principles and live the teachings of the restored Gospel of Jesus Christ and to follow in his footsteps to the best of our ability, only to encounter contention, hatred, and persecution from our nonmember families, friends, and strangers, we can't help asking, "What's wrong with Mormons?"

Appendix A: Articles of Faith

In the spring of 1842, the Prophet Joseph Smith was invited by John Wentworth, editor of the newspaper *Chicago Democrat*, to submit a statement setting forth the beliefs of the Church. Joseph originally wrote fourteen concise comprehensive declarations of Latter-day Saint beliefs. Later, revisions were made and the fourteen articles were reduced to thirteen. These declarations have come to be known as the Articles of Faith, which are given below.

The Articles of Faith of
The Church of Jesus Christ of Latter-day Saints

1. We believe in God, the Eternal Father, and in His Son, Jesus Christ, and in the Holy Ghost.

2. We believe that men will be punished for their own sins, and not for Adam's transgression.

3. We believe that through the atonement of Christ, all mankind may be saved, by obedience to the laws and ordinances of the Gospel.

4. We believe that the first principles and ordinances of the Gospel are, first, Faith in the Lord Jesus Christ; second, Repentance; third, Baptism by immersion for the remission of sins; fourth, Laying on of hands for the gift of the Holy Ghost.

5. We believe that a man must be called of God, by prophecy, and by the laying on of hands by those who are

in authority, to preach the Gospel and administer in the ordinances thereof.

6. We believe in the same organization that existed in the primitive church, namely, apostles, prophets, pastors, teachers, evangelists, and so forth.

7. We believe in the gift of tongues, prophecy, revelation, visions, healing, interpretation of tongues, and so forth.

8. We believe the Bible to be the Word of God as far as it is translated correctly; we also believe the Book of Mormon to be the Word of God.

9. We believe all that God has revealed, all that He does now reveal, and we believe that He will yet reveal many great and important things pertaining to the kingdom of God.

10. We believe in the literal gathering of Israel and in the restoration of the Ten Tribes; that Zion (the New Jerusalem) will be built upon the American continent; that Christ will reign personally upon the earth; and that the earth will be renewed and receive its paradisiacal glory.

11. We claim the privilege of worshiping Almighty God according to the dictates of our own conscience, and allow all men the same privilege, let them worship how, where, or what they may.

12. We believe in being subject to kings, presidents, rulers, and magistrates in obeying, honoring, and sustaining the law.

13. We believe in being honest, true, chaste, benevolent, virtuous, and in doing good to all men; indeed, we may say that we follow the admonition of Paul—We believe all things, we hope all things, we have endured many things, and hope to be able to endure all things. If there is anything virtuous, lovely, or of good report or praiseworthy, we seek after these things.

Appendix B: Additional Information

If you would like to have your own copy of the Book of Mormon, simply call toll-free 1-888-537-2200, and the Church will provide you with a copy at no charge to you whatsoever.

Also, if you would like a free copy of the King James Version of the Bible, you can call toll-free 1-888-537-1212.

You can also learn more about The Church of Jesus Christ of Latter-day Saints by visiting the Church's official Web sites:

www.lds.org

www.mormon.org.

You're also invited to visit the Web site:
www.whatswrongwithmormons.com

And the book's blog site:
http://whats-wrong-with-mormons.blogspot.com

Subject Index

Scripture Index

Printed in the United States
116908LV00003B/24/P

9 781583 852798